ALSO BY STEFAN THEMERSON

Bayamus (and the Theatre of Semantic Poetry)
Wooff Wooff or Who Killed Richard Wagner?
Professor Mmaa's Lecture
Cardinal Pölätüo
Tom Harris
Special Branch: A Dialogue
General Piesc (or The Case of the Forgotten Mission)
The Mystery of the Sardine
Hobson's Island

factor T
Semantic Divertissements
Logic Labels & Flesh
On Semantic Poetry
The Chair of Decency
The Urge to Create Visions

Jankel Adler or an artist seen from one of many possible angles
Kurt Schwitters in England, 1940 - 1948
Apollinaire's Lyrical Ideograms

Collected Poems

St Francis and the Wolf of Gubbio or Brother Francis' Lambchops

Mr Rouse Builds His House
The Table That Ran Away to the Woods
The Adventures of Peddy Bottom

Themerson.

CRITICS

& MY TALKING DOG

Selected Stories, Essays, Lectures & a Play

Stefan Themerson

Edited by Paul Rosheim

With an introduction by Nick Wadley

Drawings by Franciszka Themerson

BLACK SCAT BOOKS

Drawings are by Franciszka Themerson [see Notes page 228]

Cover photograph of Stefan Themerson (detail); courtesy of Idzi Rzymianin (Creative Commons License).

Cover & book design: Norman Conquest

BLACK SCAT BOOKS are published in northern California.
For additional information, please visit **BlackScatBooks.com**

For
Barbara, Jasia and Nick

CONTENTS

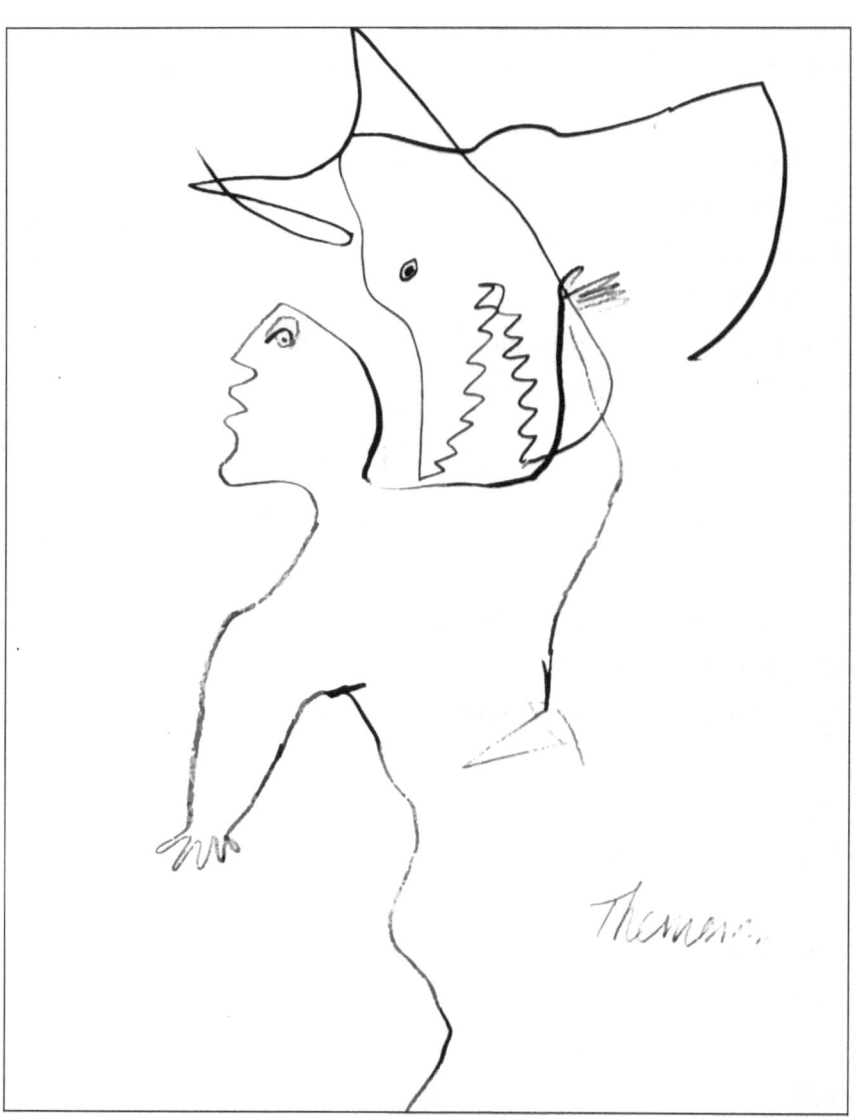

PREFACE

Shortly after I bought my first home computer in 1999, I began a series of chapbooks called Obscure Publications. I immediately and boldly contacted a literary hero of mine, Barbara Wright, the well-known British translator of Raymond Queneau, Alfred Jarry and other French luminaries, and asked if she'd kindly participate in the series. She thought that a swell idea; we enjoyed a friendly correspondence; and I found myself on her doorstep in Hampstead the following summer. Right away, she insisted on introducing me to her good friends, Jasia Reichardt and Nick Wadley, the founders and caretakers of the Themerson Archive. At that time, I hadn't heard of Stefan and Franciszka Themerson, or their legendary Gaberbocchus Press. This chance introduction, followed by my subsequent annual visits to the Archive, resulted in many delightful discoveries and experiences for me, some of which are included here.

All of the texts in this collection have appeared in OP chapbooks (in editions limited to 60 copies),[1] except for Stefan's 1957 talk, 'The Circle of Art and Science,' and the autobiographical fragments. After Stefan had completed his last novel, *Hobson's Island*, he announced that he was done writing. Nevertheless, Nick asked him what else he might have written if he hadn't made that decision. He said two things: something autobiographical; and something that would

---

1 Cunningham Memorial Library at Indiana State University maintains a complete listing of Obscure Publications chapbooks (many linked to free PDF downloads) at http://indstate.edu/about/units/rbsc/obscure/obscure.html.

gather some elements of his philosophical thoughts, so they could be further developed by someone younger. Stefan accomplished both of these things by dictating to Nick 'On fathers, wet-nurses and wars . . .' in the weeks before his death on September 6, 1988.

Some years earlier, in 1979, the Themersons turned over Gaberbocchus Press to Jaco Groot, the publisher of De Harmonie in Amsterdam. Jaco should be applauded for not only keeping much of the backlist in print but also for putting out important new books by and about the Themersons: *The Urge to Create Visions*; *Collected Poems*; *The Drawings of Franciszka Themerson*; and, most recently, *Unposted Letters: Correspondence, Diaries, Drawings, Documents 1940-1942.*[2] Similarly, the Archive was transferred to the National Library of Poland in Warsaw at the end of 2014.

Finally, I'd like to underscore the special role that Barbara Wright, Jasia Reichardt, and Nick Wadley played in my life and OP – they encouraged me, suggested projects, provided texts and scans, and invited me into their homes. I shall always be grateful for their kindnesses.

Paul Rosheim

2 In-print Gaberbocchus-De Harmonie books may be ordered online at www.gaberbocchus.nl

LINES & WORDS & THE THEMERSONS

by Nick Wadley

The remarkable range of work produced by the Themersons spanned sixty years. The earliest surviving experimental photograph by Stefan is dated 1928: the earliest surviving drawing and painting by Franciszka are each dated 1929. Their earliest collaboration was probably *Apteka* (1930), the first of five films they made together in Warsaw. The last works they made together were some sheets from the score of his opera *St Francis and the Wolf of Gubbio*, reworked for presentation to a friend in 1986. Both were working until within weeks of their deaths in 1988 – days in Stefan's case. His autobiographical fragments and his extraordinary last novel, *Hobson's Island*, were all published posthumously.

These bare facts say a great deal about the Themersons. Their work was a way of living. They spent periods that were of formative significance to both of them working in intimate collaboration, at first on their films of 1930-1945, and their books for children from the same period, and afterwards on their Gaberbocchus Press, 1948-1979. At the same time – literally at the same time, each had a rich, independent creative career. Her studio in their flat in Maida Vale, and his study along the passage, were sovereign worlds. Visits to one after the other could involve experiences that were in stark contrast.

Despite this, and despite the unusual variety of media and genres in which each worked, the most memorable characteristic that survives them lies in the degree to which they were driven by the same lasting values. As well as his novels, Stefan wrote essays on philosophy, aesthetics, semantics; canonical studies on Adler, Schwitters and Apollinaire; poems, a play and an opera. As well as making her paintings and drawings, Franciszka was an acclaimed illustrator and designer for the theatre, and her originality as a graphic designer has still to be acknowledged. Whatever they were making, and however various their artefacts may have appeared on the surface, they entertain and seduce us with comparable formal paradoxes in order to confront us, again and again, with the ambiguous crystal of the human condition.

It is not always easy to separate their respective contributions to works which they made together. Stefan told me that he couldn't do so himself in respect to their films, and it's sometimes the same with their books. In their hand-printed edition of *Aesop* (1949), credited solely to Franciszka, the hallmark of Stefan is also pervasive. The reverse is true of Stefan's canonical *Kurt Schwitters in England*. Many of Stefan's writings were illuminated by Franciszka's drawings, inseparably so. On occasion his poems were initiated by her images; on others they acted as the catalyst for her images. In the case of their *Semantic Divertissements* (1962), Stefan's hilarious text of c. 1946 was written as a commentary to a 1945 series of Franciszka's drawings, which were also to be seminal to his satirical opera, *St Francis and the Wolf of Gubbio* (1972). Their common attitude towards forms is to be found in the sort of attention they both paid to the inherent properties of whichever medium they were using.

Stefan lamented the commercial development of the camera inasmuch as it distanced the photographer from significant experience of the camera's processes. Automation and conditions that are preset by the manufacturer took the photographer's finger away from the camera's pulse. In a similar way, he said that the first talkies had put at risk the integrity of film, inasmuch as the medium was dragged towards emulation of theatre. He singled out Vigo's *L'Atalante* as embodying a complete, unadulterated sense of the medium, and as a lasting model for the future. Both he and Franciszka were urgently concerned with the film, art and writing of the next generation.

Franciszka used a prodigal range of materials for drawing: pencils, chalks, crayons, inks and paints. The apparently effortless fluency of her execution speaks of her intimate ease with each medium. She coaxed from each what was in its character to do most eloquently. A change of medium involved whole change, sometimes in a single drawing. In her *Calligrammes* of 1960-61, the drawings comprise paint that is poured, dripped, run or scraped across the paper: extravagantly gestural, and yet with incidents of great refinement. Her *Traces of Living*, a long series of drawings between 1960 and 1967, involved a different sort of improvisation, in that the linear perambulations across each sheet become conspiracies. From each perambulation of her apparently guileless pen-drawn line emerge eyes, faces, hands, silhouettes, whose clear if ambiguous identities manage not to compromise the integrity of the line. Working in paint on canvas was effectively another form of drawing for her. She celebrated the sensuality of the medium – much of the paint is larded on with a palette knife – but the images are usually formed from incised lines and edges. Her colour was rubbed or stained onto the paint surface rather than being part of it.

Franciszka's intimate identification with her line may well be likened to Stefan's feeling for the word: for its proper meaning, its music, its typographic disposition. His shrewd insights into the work of Schwitters and Apollinaire are revealing manifestations. His invention of semantic poetry, while explaining as the stripping of a poem to expose the reality behind it, in practice became the platform for a good deal of extravagant and often very funny improvisation. This duality is visible throughout his poems, essays and novels. He loved the exactness and clarity of the English language, as well as its more elusive and oblique properties. He also savoured the musical structures of language, repetition and alliteration, in prose as much as in poems.

It isn't particularly rewarding to discuss for very long the forms of the Themersons' work without the content for which they were a vehicle. Anyone who has read the least thing about the Gaberbocchus Press is likely to have come across Stefan's declared ambition for it: to produce not best sellers, but 'best lookers'. They published 57 titles between 1948 and 1979, and their books are indeed original and seductive in their design. What begs for attention is how different they look, one from another. The germ of each book was formed and nurtured by the nature of its content, the variety of typography, illustrations, format and paper from one book to another is formidable. Close analysis reveals very quickly how much the form was determined by the subject. When economy demanded a more modest format in the later years of the Press, they evolved a cool house style which did not impose itself on the content. As well as affording an outlet for their own work, the founding intention of the Press was to make available unpublished work by continental writers, and new works by younger English writers. They published first English translations of Jarry, Queneau, Pol-Dives, Grabbe, Stern;

the work of Schwitters, Apollinaire, Jankel Adler, Raoul Hausmann, Henri Chopin; as well as Bertrand Russell, Stevie Smith, C.H. Sisson, Oswell Blakeston, Kenneth Tynan, and others.

They emerged from a Polish avant-garde which had reconciled in its embrace Constructivist and Dadaist tendencies. Their own work contained extremes both of outraged protest and pure abstraction. Compared to the 1943-44 film *Calling Mr Smith*, their next and last film *The Eye and the Ear* (1945) might seem a purely aesthetic affair, as might the more abstract of Franciszka's drawings. But this very range of their activities – their refusal to accept conventional categories; their constant breaking of boundaries, mixing of media – constitutes a unified statement about individual liberties, about the freedom to walk backwards. In this sense their lives' work may be seen to hold homogeneous moral and political values. Their targets embraced the mindless institutions of the modern world: clichés of thought, behavior and social structure. These were scrutinised and debunked in the clear light of common sense and individual human identity. When asked once what were the strengths and weaknesses of Gaberbocchus Press, Stefan gave the same answer for both: 'refusal to conform'.

He would not have appreciated being called a moralist, but the ultimate implication of their works is never far from the concepts of good and evil. A recurrent theme of Stefan's writing was that we are born with inbred, biological instincts that enable us to behave with decency towards each other. We only lose these values, he says, because we become successively conditioned by faiths, beliefs and causes – whether religious, nationalistic, political or technological. Around the tyrants and fanatics of Franciszka's drawings revolves a world of little men who conform mindlessly to the current faith. It is no coincidence that she responded with such brilliant graphic imagination (and through five successive versions for page or stage, 1951-1970) to the grotesque and timeless fable of Jarry's *Ubu Roi*; nor that both of them identified so readily with the anarchic emancipation of nonsense of their friend Kurt Schwitters. The Themersons lie in direct succession to that modern tradition. They sang the same music of hilarity and the ridiculous, with lyrics that range from savagery to velvet satire. Their entire oeuvres, independent and collaborative, treat matters of gravity with a seductive levity.

ESSAYS

THE AIM OF AIMS

I

You asked me to read to you. This invitation, so nice and flattering, made me go to a park and sit on a bench and reflect, made me walk through the streets and reflect, made me lie on my couch and reflect, and the reflection, both melancholy and not sad, was like the hand of a watch, moving round and round and round, always forward, and always coming back to its point of departure. Hence melancholy, because questioning is the essence of progress.

I wanted to grow a crystal, and bring it to you as a gift. I wanted to wrap it nicely in words, and give it to you tonight. Alas … and it is not that I'm not capable of putting forms in symmetries of rhymes and rhythms … but crystals grow from undisputed tranquility, and this I couldn't find in myself.

Thus, I got up from my bench, I stopped in the middle of the pavement, I jumped out of my dream: What I shall bring you is a flaming torch, a loudhailer, an *Allons, Citoyens!* Fortunately … and it is not that I'm not capable of putting rhymes and rhythms into a howling cry … but, having lived through hairpin bends in History, and met and seen and heard some howling voices, both true and false (of which the former – more dangerous) – I called my sense of humour to stop me, just in time.

Thus, I have come to you tonight empty-handed, having no offerings of Aims to give, because no Aim is so exalted that it be worth a heartbeat more than Decency of Means. Because, when all is said and done, Decency of Means *is* the aim of aims.

II

Some naive lovers of semantics believe that if only our rulers, our saviours (of all sorts), could understand the meaning of their own pronouncements, they would amend their ways. What an illusion! They, the saviours, know the mechanism of Language much better than all the Semanticists, Linguistic philosophers, and Logical formalists put together. That's how they know how to use it to play upon the prejudices of the mob: you and me.

And, when a Poet, or a Novelist, becomes a Demagogue, the same applies to him. Because POETRY, as well as POLITICS, may be morally *vicious*, and intellectually *dishonest*. In such cases, both poetry and oratory – political, religious, philosophical – are like crime: The greater a crime is, the more impressive it is, but the less excusable.

Thus, when all is said and done, one finds that no poetic rhymes, no greatness, no philosophical systems, no reasons of state, no politic ends, and no utopian aims are more important than decency of means. Because, when all is said and done, decency of means *is* the aim of aims.

III

And here, straight from the lopped and barked wood of bare trunks, come some classical formalists, who dream their dream about the world of distinct nouns and predicates, governed by the yes-or-no law of the excluded middle, the world in which things (including you and me and him and her) are what they are, and are not what they are not. And they dream their dreams to their logical conclusions, in an airtight Festschrift, or on a broad canvas: religious, economic, political. And when we feel not at our ease in their dream, they say: "You must believe us, because our assumptions are good, and our logic is true, and if you don't see it working, it's because our dreams have never been tried."

Which is not as it is. All dreams have been tried. And all have worked – partly. And all have not worked – partly. And they worked not – whenever their sires and seers, and the successors of the sires and seers, believed that if their assumptions are good, and their logic is true, then the conclusions become aims, and all methods can be used to achieve them; that the end justifies the means.

In which, their faultless formal axiomatic logic omits two facts: ONE: that in this changing world, the way from premises to conclusions is temporal and stormy, and you can't force your yesterday upon your grandsons' tomorrow; TWO: that using wicked means for the sake of aims defeats the aims.

Now, let us not get ourselves sidetracked by academic questions: how to define what is not definable by definition: how to define "wicked" and how to define "decent". As if we didn't know what we mean when we use these words, however differently we use them. As if the reality of the emotive force that is in us was less real than the confused reality of things to which these undefinabilities refer.

Thus, whatever your notions of the wicked and of the decent are, whatever is the practical use you make of them, even if your aims are good only for some chosen group caste class faith, race or nation, and to the detriment of all the rest of us, the wickedness of your means will destroy your aims, because, even for the wickedest logician, the aim of aims is some sort of decency of means.

IV

As you see, my Logic is not axiomatic. She doesn't march forward, goose-step by goose-step, from indubitable truths to indisputable consequences, from arbitrary principles to conclusions unchecked by results, uncontrolled by the output, deaf to the feedback of reality. It is empirical evidence, rather than theoretical prejudice, that has shaped her body, and guided her syllogisms.

Looking backwards over her shoulder, from the results towards reasons, which were the results of previous reasons, she may never arrive at first principles, but, somewhere half-way along the chain of events, half-way between Man and the first nucleic acid molecules replicating themselves, she comes across a fact; not across a truth, but across a fact. The very simple fact. The fact that of all possible species of carnivora, those only survived, whose everhungry members did *not* devour their own children before the children grew up and produced the next and next and next carnivorous generation.

This illogical behaviour, which allowed the species to continue, you may call "a biological fact", or you may call it "altruism", or – why not? – love. If you call it "a biological fact", then it's physics. If you call it "love" then it's ethics. And, in the cruel world, in which the beast had to attack to feed not only himself but also his litter, this biological fact, this logical absurdity, this seed of ethics, – "love", must have preceded aggression (which, paradoxically, it caused) and decency must have preceded wickedness.

As time marches on, this logical absurdity of caring not only for himself makes the beast enlarge the field of decency from the litter to the pack, the tribe, race, class, nation, – the whole species? Anyway, such a sequence of events is what I would like to call "progress". And I would like to think that it is carried forward not by beliefs in fetishes, not by Great Illusions, not by aggression (WHICH, FROM BEING AGGRESSION FOR THE SAKE OF FOOD, DEGENERATED INTO AGGRESSION FOR THE SAKE OF IDEAS), but by its own evolutionary momentum, in spite of our cultural push-pulls, exercised by Grand Aims, noble or wicked.

When my Logic looks backwards over her shoulder, she sees that the absence of wicked means is more important than the presence of Grand Aims.

And when she turns around and glances forward into the future, what she sees is the urgent need for the food of common decencies, which will grow not from the aggressive nightmares of bygones, not from the glorious blue-prints for the morrow, but from the common decencies of now.

MAN'S SUPERIORITY TO THE BEASTS

It was in the French film, "La Femme du Boulanger": a dialogue written by a poet Jean Giono, a dialogue between the parson and the teacher in a little village in Provence. The ambassador of Church reproached the ambassador of Science for having told the children that Jeanne D'Arc *believed* she heard the voices of Heaven. He ought to have said: She *did* hear them. But then the teacher reproached the parson for having told the children that God made *four* kingdoms of Nature: Mineral, Vegetable, Animal, and Human. The teacher knew but three Kingdoms: Mineral, Vegetable, and Animal.

My personal feelings are with the teacher and I believe the subject of this discussion ought to be not Man's superiority to the beasts, but Man's superiority to the *other* beasts. But even in this form one word seems to need better definition. The word: *superiority*.

I understand that nobody has in mind Man's superiority in *running,* for instance, in which we cannot compare with the hare; or superiority of sense of *orientation,* in which Man is beaten easily by the pigeon, or of sense of *organization,* in which the bees are so much superior to us; or the capacity for *regeneration,* which seems to be greater among the amphibians, salamanders, and lizards; or superiority in the *expression of emotion in love,* in which Man can't compare with the deer. Neither shall we use such words as *superiority of soul,* if we don't want to make the subject meaningless and nonsensical for every Logical Positivist. Unless we mean by the superiority of soul the observable *complexity of Man's emotional life* and *superiority of his intellectual powers,* which, in our time, is not so big as to give us the definite answer concerning the intellectual powers of animals. In this case we may deal with it in more than a couple of different ways.

We may *feel* it like St. Francis of Assisi or like Fox-Hunting Man, we may *think* like Bergson or *believe* like theologians, we may *synthesize* our ideas, like poets or painters, and we may try to *know,* to know the real truth – and here, real means observable, we may try it with the scientists who in their work refer not to the authority of their own prejudices or to those of the past ages, but to the authority of Nature.

But one thing we may say with all the certitude and without the help of scientific laboratories is that *even* if all the philosophers *think,* all the prophets *believe,* all the common people *feel,* all the painters *paint,* all the poets *sing,* all the scientists *prove,* that the Soul of the Ox and the Spirit of the Fly are superior to ours – we won't stop eating beefsteaks or using fly-swats. We will never worship the Cow, not because our soul, as we define it, is superior to that of cows, but because we with our bows, rifles, and sulfonamides are *stronger* than them. If we are all a race of high-spirited saints and the insects are but soul-less machines, it will be they who are "ultimate victors on the earth". "Perhaps" – as said Bertrand Russell – "from a cosmic point of view this is not to be regretted; but as a human being I cannot help heaving a sigh over my own species".

Certainly it will be very happy for us if it will be proved that we have in ourselves something noble and different from matter, and the other animals haven't. Education would be a lighter task and to write a book of Ethics would be as easy as writing, for instance, *Mein Kampf.* The only difference would be there, where now end the Superman and begin other Aryan branches in a New Book, would end Man, and would begin Ape; that there, where in *Mein Kampf* end the other races and begin the lower of the lowest – a Jew, there in a New Book would begin the sub-kingdom, unprotected by the Fellowship of Animals' Friends – of the unicellular Protozoa. There is a temptation here to conclude that the *superiority argument* absolves us from our imperialism over Nature. We very often reproach the dog for not being able to understand us literally. But we ourselves do not understand the language (if we dare call it so) of, for instance, the termites. What shall we do with our superiority argument if it would happen one day to be proved by the professors of Cambridge that the banging by the termites against the walls of their cities is nothing but worship of the Almighty?

One might say that all this talk of the superiority of our soul (whatever it might be) is necessary for the practical purpose of Education. But that's hypocrisy. I might imagine that some degree of hypocrisy may be not only necessary but even fruitful if it successfully serves the bad teacher to appear before the class as a good example to imitate. But it isn't easy to believe in any honest education constrained to call for arguments that are only metaphysical hypocrisy. One of the consequences of such an education is arrogance and pride that is inculcated by the generations of teachers into generations of school children, and thus made an inherited characteristic of our time in Europe. I mentioned, at the beginning of this perhaps too long speech, the parson and the teacher from the French film. It's in the parson, believing himself to be in God's Image, who stated with all his authority that the kingdom of Man is separate from that of Animals, that I find all the haughtiness, arrogance, and pride, and in the teacher, that I find modesty, discretion, temperance and, I'm tempted to say, Christian humility.

I'm sure that our teacher doesn't like cruelty to animals any more than the parish priest, although he doesn't refer to any authority. It is independent of religious and metaphysical speculations that none of us like cruelty to animals. But, I suspect, it's not as much for their sake as for ours. We don't like blood on our hands. But since we must have it incessantly, we are used to saying: "Well, if it is necessary". If it is necessary for our sake, not for that of animals. One might go further and say that if we don't like to make ourselves bloodthirsty heroes, this very fact is due to the centuries of religious education. But if I say "we" I do not mean "men". I mean *some* men. Because some others, who have Two Thousand Years of Christianity behind them, *do* like cruelty to beasts, still more if those beasts belong to the order, Primates.

CADAQUÉS

On the top of a hill in Cadaqués, there is a church with a sundial on which you can read the words:

Jo sense sol,
tu sense Fe,
no valem res.

One summer afternoon I met a priest there who, after a preliminary conversation about mucho viento, asked me what my religion was. On the spur of the moment I told him I was a logical positivist. As he had never heard of such a denomination and it was now too late for me to back out, I had to tell him something about it. I mentioned Russell as its Spring and Forefather, and Ayer as its Thomas Aquinas. I'm afraid he didn't know the first two names. He was most anxious to learn whether logical positivism was a Christian denomination or not, and relaxed visibly when told it was not – if it was not Christian then, thank God, it was ignorant of the Truth and therefore there was no room for heresy in it. He sat beside me on the low white, sun-hot wall, some hundred feet above the level of the sea. "And what does your teaching say about the immortality of the soul?" he asked.

Well, there I was, invited to drink down the brew I had inadvertently prepared for myself. "We," I said, not feeling at all at my ease, firstly because I had labeled myself one of the clan of logical positivists, and secondly because I was usurping the role of their spokesman. "We don't particularly mind what kind of signs people use to draw a map of the world so long as it helps them to find their place in it. If they choose to give a certain set of circumstances the name of 'soul', I don't see why they shouldn't."

"A certain set of circumstances?" he repeated, lifting up his thick black brows and taking the heavy Spanish cigarette out of his mouth. "How can 'a certain set of circumstances' be immortal?"

"Well," I said, "why not? After all, what *is* the duration of a set of circumstances? When does it begin, when does it end? Doesn't what we think of its duration depend on the meaning we human beings give to its temporal identity? The keyword is 'continuity'. Any duration is no longer than, let's say, of a second, if that: and if we do accept the notion of continuity, 'mortality' will be more difficult to understand than 'immortality'."

"What I am asking is," he said, "whether you believe that your set of circumstances will survive your death?"

"Well," I said, "what we have so far agreed to is that it is not non-sensical to say that there is continuity between that set of circumstances which you would prefer to call 'my soul at 3.30 p.m. today', and, let's say, that set of circumstances which you would prefer to call 'my soul at 3.30 p.m. tomorrow'. The question you are asking now is: will it still make sense to talk about that 24-hours' portion of continuity if I happen to die at midnight? But surely the answer to that question depends on the standards employed by the inquirer, and the standards he employs depend on the purpose of his inquiry. If he doesn't say 'any change (however small) in the set of circumstance discontinues it', then he must choose what the amount of change would be that would allow us to regard the set as discontinued. And that choice is arbitrary, it depends on him, on his purpose. He may regard my soul before I met you half an hour ago as so different from what it will have become in, say, another half hour, as to warrant him to regard them as two different things. On the other hand, for some different purpose, he may regard the set of circumstances of today and that of tomorrow as one continuous thing, even if I die in the meantime."

He squashed between his fingers the burning end of the cigarette he was smoking, and said: "The important thing is that you admit that it makes sense to say that the set of circumstances exists and undergoes changes. Don't you?"

"Indeed I do", I said.

"Then," he asked, "wouldn't you and your logical positivists agree that if it changes it ought to change for the better?"

I reflected for a moment. Then I answered: "I think it would be correct for me to say that all the logical positivists I have happened to come across were trying to change for the better those of their sets of circumstances which you would call their souls. None of them, however, would or could demonstrate an argument showing that they *ought* to do so.

"Never mind the arguments," he said. "The point is that if it moves towards good then, surely, it comes from evil."

"I don't like your terms", I objected, "'evil' is a word that has personal ..."

"Now, now," he interrupted me, "haven't you noticed that whenever you wanted to be understood clearly, you yourself have been using my terms and not yours? When you wanted to make clear what kind of set of circumstances you were talking about in your terms, you used *my* terms and you said (as you had to say), – 'soul'. You used *my* terms, and you had to use them. You had nothing against using the word 'soul' when you wanted to make clear what you were talking about, neither did you shrink from the expression 'change for the better'."

"Touché," I said.

"This is not a duel," he said.

"Touché again," I said, and felt foolish. "Sorry," I said. "Of course this is not a duel."

"Let's resume our positions," he said. "We seem to have agreed that the set of circumstances which I call the soul is capable of changing from what I, with your permission, call evil. Therefore as we seem to agree that it holds in itself some goodness at the end of the journey which you may call an evolutionary process, and some evil at its beginning . . ."

"Wait a moment," I said. "You talk about evil as if it were a bit of an insect embedded in a lump of solid amber. I haven't agreed to that. I don't think that what we call 'evil' is in what we call 'soul'. On the contrary, I think it is around it. It is in the fabric of the whole world, the living world, and not in those particular sets of circumstances which you call 'the soul'."

"My son," he said, "you think you are very far from the faith, in fact, you are very near it."

"Father," I answered, "you are making a mistake. I am as far from your faith as you are from my views. We may be no more than two feet apart, but there is a wall between us, and it may be easier to go round the earth and meet somewhere on the antipodes than to pierce that wall. You believe that we possess our moral code because it was given to us, or imposed on us, by an Outside Power. I think that we have found ourselves in possession of it because dead bodies stink."

"They do," he said.

"And men don't like the stink of dead bodies."

"True," he replied, and added reflectively:

"A slight whiff of the smell they may like, especially if mixed with the smell of incense. But there is a limit to it, I agree."

"So there we are," I said. "Beyond the limit you mention, man's nose happens to be negatively chemotropic to the stimulus of that kind of smell. It turns away from, and tries to escape and not to be caught by, the gaseous molecules and minute solid particles emanating from dead bodies. However, the world around man's nose, the world around his hungry stomach, is such that he finds it necessary to kill and produce dead bodies. I don't say that he minds killing. I say that he doesn't like smelling. This is the essence of his conflict. He was in the position of a child who held his nose when taking a spoonful of cod liver oil. It was to hold his nose against the offensive smell of putrefaction that man invented his Religions and his Ethical Codes. If he could eat all of his kill before it got decomposed, if he himself always died in the odour of sanctity, he would never have invented any of your Ten Commandments. Why should he? We can invent reasons why he should, but we are the result of what he had already done. He had no reason to invent the reasons we can invent for him now. No reason at all. Except that smell. Is that not why our civilizations come from Mediterranean and other stinking lands where putrefaction happens to be favourised by the climate? In hotter parts you have hosts of insects and small animals who undertake the job, and you have aerobic processes that oxidize the remains. At the North Pole you have natural refrigeration. Yet in Madrid, in Rome, in Athens, in Mecca, in Jerusalem, in Calcutta, proteins split into dust by an anaerobic process, with the formation of foul-smelling, incompletely oxidized products of bacteria and fungi. Listen, Father. At the beginning of civilization a new type of nervous system mutated into being. Like all the other nervous systems that had been crowding the earth, it still possessed a positive reaction to food. At the same time, however, and unlike the others, it had a negative reaction to the minute quantities of incompletely oxidized molecules radiating from the decomposed proteins. To help itself in this conflict of positive and negative tropisms appearing simul-

taneously, the upper part of the nervous system invented Civilization, at the end of which it invented not only refrigeration to retard
the decomposition of dead bodies, but also hermetically sealed gas
chambers, flame throwers oxidizing proteins *in vivo,* and smelless,
clean, atomic bombs. Thus civilization has invented the means of
suppressing what once upon a time gave it its birth. Don't you see
that we make less fuss today about the hygienically liquidated,
smelless millions than Agamemnon did about the single body of
his daughter, which would have to start smelling before the sun had
reached the meridian? No, it is by Deodorizing Death, and not by
Atheism that our Civilization is in the process of committing suicide."

"Are you serious?" he asked.

"A leg-pull that is consistent is a serious matter," I said. "More serious than a philosophical or theological system that lacks consis-
tency. Do you not see that by my trying to show that, meek as they
are, physical factors *are* capable of producing ethical values, I aim at
building up the Rock where, so far, we have nothing better than the
authority of your conviction?"

"Well," he said, "but even if I accept your theory, you still won't be
able to disprove that the giving of those two, positive and negative,
reflexes to the nervous system was the means God chose to teach
the nervous system His Ethics."

"Look, Father," I said, at the same time realising that he could
have been my son – "Please don't think that I am so keen on
disproving your God, I am no more interested in disproving Him
than in disproving a neutrino. You try to explain bricks by describing
houses, houses for you are bits of towns, kingdoms explain the
existence of your towns, the gestalt of the earth explains the gestalt
of your kingdoms, and God explains the earth. Scientists do exactly
the same things, only they go in the opposite direction. For them,
bits of wood explain the chair they sit on, molecules explain the bits

of wood, atoms explain the molecules, and particles or packets of energy explain the atoms. It may be that scientists predict better where the moon will rise again, and that you predict better what the man you have just confessed will do tomorrow. Nevertheless you both try to use Occam's razor. *Entia non sunt multiplicanda praeter necessitatem*. There you seem to be even more efficient than your opposite number, the scientist. He can't reduce the number of his fundamental constants below seven; you have succeeded in reducing them to four."

"Four?" he interrupted.

"Four," I said. "True, a long time ago you made a mental effort in reducing the number to one fundamental constant, God. But you saw that the system wasn't consistent and you had to admit a second, the Devil; but the system wasn't consistent and you had to admit the Son; but the system wasn't consistent and you had to admit the Holy Spirit. I don't say that the system has become consistent, but I admit that it gave you some freedom of manipulation. Nevertheless, whatever is the origin of the Foul Odour we are talking about, wherever it comes from, whether it comes from God sitting on the top of your ladder or from the scientist's molecules, it is not its origin but it itself that is responsible for our inventing the things we call moral codes, or ethics."

He came nearer. We were again sitting on the white wall at the top of the precipice, and for a moment I thought that he intended to push me over it. Alone as we were there, in the village of Cadaqués he would have had thirty witnesses to prove his innocence. Instead, he stood up, bent over me and said:

"Sir," he said, "even if it were true, as I don't think it is, even if our ethics came not from God but from the offensive odour of dead bodies, we should go on making people think that it came from Above. Wherever it came from, we two, you and I, we like it, our moral code, don't we? Now, if we go on making people think what I believe is true, namely that it came from Above, it will have a chance to survive. After all, my system, inefficient as it may be, I admit, does still work. On the other hand, if you tell people that their Ethics comes from where you think it does . . . Lord Jesus! You don't know what scientists are! They will invent a universal anti-stink. And what shall we do with our souls?"

"We shall have none," I said. "Negative tropisms, the fact of possessing a nervous system which makes us flee from the stink produced by decomposing proteins, shortly: The Dislike of The Smell of Dead Bodies, is a necessary part of the definition of Man. If scientists ever change that property of our nervous system, if we ever come to like the smell, we shall be men no more. And then you will not need to worry about us any more than you do about hyenas or hedgehogs. And don't look at me like that, please," I said. "It is not I who invented the world as I find it."

The bright, fiery sun was burning above our heads, the stinking ruins of the village fell away down the slope of the hill towards the blue of the sea. On the other side of the bay, Salvador Dali was waxing his moustaches in a whitewashed room asphyxiated with the pungent smell of fifty, fully-open, yellow-centred white lilies.

"What you say is horrid," the priest said.

"I know it is," I said.

"How can you carry the burden of such a philosophy without being comforted by the thought of . . ."

I interrupted him: "The thought of there being one *more* Person who died for me would only add weight to the burden."

"But he did die for you." This time the priest didn't sound sincere, and I kept silent.

"When you want to come," he pointed to the door of the church – "I will be there, waiting."

"Not before I lose my battle," I said, "and sink into the mood in which any acquired truth that gives peace is welcome," and in all decor our dialogue didn't sound operatic at all, or perhaps I should say that it did, but that that wasn't out of place in the circumstances.

He jumped on to his motor bike, gave it a kick, made the sign of the cross, and went off.

SKETCHES FROM A POLITE HELL

Suidecidedly decide I to break through bloody, a bloody, the bloody linglish linguistic langousta, the last word of which statemently battlecry will sound ludicrous in the hearens of those who don't know that there is a lango in which usta means mouth, in my case a mouth full of twisted red flesh bulging under the roof vulgo palate and bathing its rose tip in the miniature sea of saliva, pressing and prezzing and prething against rows of white plastic, blastic, mlastic, iconoclastic teeth guarded by two dry lipbms, upper lipf and lower libv, upper limb and lover limf, and arching forward and forwant and forwarn and backhwardz and bequewarts and beghworts, and upwalds and upwarrtz, filling the whole mouth with its swollenness, the whole hole of the mouth with its red tumenascent beefsteakedness, all wet and barring the passage of bvreath from the larynx, to produce the unheard distinctions between bad and bed, between black call and telephone coal, between Miss John Smith and Mr. Joan Smith, and the fibre of the sound rebounces off and back into my gullet rejected by the feardrum of the native listener who cannot classify it as belonging to, as belonging in, as coming from, as ffallen offf off any step of the ladder in any county of the United Kingdom or the United States, of Canada or Ghana, of India or New Zealand, and when the behaviourist movements of the red meat in my mouth are windless and, leaving the air alone, guide my hand which pencils mute black signs on a piece of paper, then it is not the membrane of his ear but the cornea of his eye that rejects the scribble scrible, because the scribble scrible is neither Partridge nor Oxbridge, neither pidgin nor Ogden and richin, and therewherefromm has to be put aside like the corpse of an acquaintance of an unknown passerby, because whatsoever does not blong to, or blong in, exists not. What other pooff of existence may there be, you think, except blonging?

ON FATHERS, WET-NURSES AND WARS...

I. MY FATHER

When I started to think about it, it struck me that I know so little: I'm not even sure when he was born. Some calculations suggest that it was 1872, but it may be that it was a year later or earlier. He finished at the gymnasium – what in my youth was Malachowski's (but what was its name in the nineteenth century?). Then the University of Medicine in Warsaw, *summa cum laude*. I know he visited London and Paris, probably in 1910; I was under the impression that it was to hear the lectures of Charcot, but that was impossible because Charcot died in 1893. In any case, it was under the influence of Charcot that he became interested in medical hypnotism. (His eyes were green and obstinate. He used improvisation – 'clouds . . . sky . . . wind . . .' – as if poetical improvisation could submerge his patients' depression.)

Already before the First World War there were in his consulting-room guinea pigs, a microscope, the electrostatic machine of Winshurst, a pantostat, some infra-red lamps, and – after the war – the ultra-violet lamp, etc. He liked to call himself a doctor devoted to hygiene, or a doctor devoted to social problems. He was a school doctor and (before the war) a doctor to the fire service. And I think he had something to do as well with the supply of water to the community. I remember seeing once a copy of the humorous weekly *Mucha* – also before the First World War – in which there was a satire on two Polish pioneer hygienists, Doctor Tchórznicki (if my memory doesn't mislead me) and Doctor Themerson.

In 1904, as a military doctor, he took part in the war with Japan, somewhere out in the East (?Manchuria). He wrote at the time a short story called *Manza*. Bolesław Prus congratulated him (in a letter of 1906). The story was published in *Tygodnik Ilustrowany*, I believe in the same year, 1906, and later on, in a collection of short stories under the same title, *Manza,* printed in 1927 by F. Pauli, Grodzka 6, Płock. I know that somewhere around then, at the start of the century, two of his plays were staged in a theatre in Łódź (I don't know why in Łódź), with Władysław(?) Tartarkiewicz(?) so far as I remember. This information I saw in one of the editions of the Olgebrand Encyclopedia. I think those plays were written under the influence of Zapolska, whom he knew personally.

Of those days, from before the First World War (and even before I was born), I can quote an 'historic' anecdote which shows his civic courage. After he had come back from the Japanese war, he was standing in his consulting-room one day and saw through the window, in Grodzka [street], that a soldier of the tsar was whipping a Jew (the Jew was dressed in the traditional long coat). My father left his patient, put on his officer's greatcoat, ran downstairs and ordered the soldier to report to his command (I think it was in the Plac Kanoniczny). The outcome was rather comical because my father had gone out into the street without his belt on, and for that offence he was sentenced to three weeks in the fortress in Warsaw. That fortress couldn't have been too tragic, because – I remember – my mother's teasing commentary was: 'wine, women and song'. So far as 'wine' was concerned, I shouldn't think so since (in my time at least) he didn't drink, didn't smoke. 'Women' – of yes! 'Song'? When he was young he played the violin, although I never saw him with a violin in his hands, but he was musical in a sentimental way. There was no gramophone in the house because at the time a gramophone was something vulgar. But there was the piano, an upright. On that same piano, my mother once had to play Chopin's Funeral March while my father recited Kornel Ujejski's poem. The occasion was the day on which we had learned, by telegraph from Paris, of the suicide of my mother's niece, wife of a Bergsonian philosopher. I revolted against the performance. But that was what he was like:

emotionally – sentimentally romantic;
stylistically – naïvely baroque;
morally – classically dogmatic;
in the conduct of his life – an unpractical realist.

A rather strange amalgam, but perhaps in some sense rather typical of the passage from the nineteenth century into the twentieth century. About Chopin, perhaps things were not as simple as they seemed to me (in the twenties), because in his waiting-room there was hanging an enormous engraving in a wide black frame called 'Chopin improvising in a Parisian salon'. It had a hand-written dedication 'To Mieczysław Themerson' as a memento, but without a signature. But I knew that it was a gift from a legendary Miss Zofja.

1914. The New War – and again as a military doctor, eastwards. This time the whole family (my mother; my brother, who was at the time 14; my sister, 9; and I, 4) followed him eastwards to be at the same side of the moving battle lines. Riga, St Petersburg (or rather, Petrograd), Wielkie Łuki. I didn't see him much at this time because he was mostly at the hospitals at the front, but in the last town, Wielkie Łuki, he must have been together with us, because I remember that his batman was a 'governess' to me. He (the *denshchyk* [Russian for batman]) must have come from somewhere far away. A conscripted *mushik*. The proud possessor of a miraculous pencil: it was blue at one end and red at the other. With it, he drew lines and lines of little blue rectangles on wheels pulled by a red steam locomotive, showing his ever-present nostalgia. The Western world was quite new to him. When he was given some macaroni (or was it spaghetti?), he thought they were white worms and told the cook; 'and the white worms are quite tasty'. He used to take me to a green hill at the outskirts of the town, where some ages before, a Polish king won a battle with the Russians. He would lift me up and make me sit on a sort of pillar that was there. And he sang 'Ta-ra-ra-boom-di-ay, I'm sitting on a pillar, A policeman came up and he took me home.' It was ages later that I found the 'ta-ra-ra-boom-di-ay' in Gilbert & Sullivan. It seems that our culture in the form of 'ta-ra-ra-boom-di-ay' is spreading round the world much faster than our gastronomy in the form of spaghetti and macaroni.

We came back to Poland in the autumn of 1918 by a train called *Ciepłuszka* [to do with warmth, literally] through Wilno, Warsaw and back to Płock, to the same apartment (Grodzka 5), which of course I had not remembered. The apartment and consulting-room survived, but so far as I knew there was no money at all, because I remember that when I was sent for the first time to the primary school, I went there in my sister's cap and other children were making fun of me. So the next day it was necessary to buy me the proper school cap on credit. And thus, in spite of the gossip that everybody who comes back from Russia comes back with diamonds from tsar's crown, my father had to start from the beginning to earn our living. He wasn't interested in party politics, but his interest in social affairs came back to him immediately, because already as soon as 1919 – or was it 1920? – someone denounced him as a Bolshevik. He was taken to prison in a horse-driven black maria (iron wheels on the cobble-stones). Even many years later, whenever that kind of vehicle trundled along Grodzka during the night, my mother would wake up and run to the window. The times were stormy and dangerous. Capital punishment was not such a rarity. My mother went to Warsaw, where a Mr Szyszkowski was a procurator-general, who had also been at Wielkie Łuki when we were there. There, together, he and my father were organizing the 200th anniversary of the death of General Kościuszko. It must have been a curious picture: my father in the uniform of a tsar's officer, with a Order of St Stanislas on his breast, celebrating Kościuszko's anniversary and reciting his poems in the naïve style of Konopnicka. Mr Szyszkowski intervened to say that the accusation was without foundation, that it was malicious because my father was a Polish patriot even in Russia. Well, that intervention was successful and he was freed without delay. But the whole incident was very painful for him; for instance, he liked to go in the evenings to Mr Skowroński's café on Plac Kanoniczny. But something unpleasant must have happened there (or perhaps the man who denounced him used to go there), because my father transferred his evenings to the Szalański café on Tumska Street, which was less old-fashioned.

Whether the question of the so-called *Czarny Dwór* ['black place' or 'black spot'] started before 1920 or later I don't know, but it lasted for years. My father brought an initiative to build housing (council houses) for the unemployed there. There had been much spiteful opposition, but finally the houses were built (1924?), I went one day to see them, since I'd heard so much about it, and they struck me as a series of miserable, low, gloomy, wooden buildings – was it necessary to fight so many battles to succeed in building such affairs? All the same, it was a real social achievement: not a poetical literary achievement, but one that was tangibly real. I know that there was a proposal to name the little street after my father, but the proposal failed because the council decided that the little street was too miserable.

Of what he had written after the First World War, the most interesting was perhaps *The Martyrology of the School Doctor*, printed as a series in *Pogłosy Szkolne*. He also wrote for the weekly – or was it fortnightly? – journal of which the offices were on Tumska Street (*Tygodnik Polski*? – I don't remember the title). He signed his pieces '*Prawdzic*' (Of Truth). Late in the evening, after his work and after his session in the café, he would work on a novel, which appeared in Cracow in 19??, under the title *Bunt Krwi* (The Revolt of the Blood) (copies exist in Poland). My mother used to say that an unpleasant review of it contributed to his death; he was rather proud, he wouldn't tolerate the affront.

When Mr Liszewski, the history teacher, decided to keep me back a year at school – because my memory when I was young was still worse than it is today: I couldn't recite all the Polish kings chronologically with their dates, and, at a distance from the map, I confused Kurlandja and Inflanty (Balkan states) – my father met with Mr Liszewski in the Szalański café and came to a gentleman's agreement, which meant that I would be allowed to pass up to the fifth form, but would not attend school for a whole year. And that's how it was. [Stefan explained that although there was an implicit understanding that he would be privately educated, this was not so; during that year he built his first radio set, with a large aerial on the roof, and made his first excursions into photography. He also spent two months or so in a sanatorium at Zakopane, since his parents were concerned that, like his brother, he may contract TB.]

My mother loved and admired my father. This wasn't an easy thing for her to do, since her family despised him sardonically, first because the dowry he received was dissipated instead of building a solid material career, secondly that he spoilt his life with his quixotry (which, nevertheless, they could not help but be impressed by). He used to get up at 8; before 9 he was already in his consulting-room waiting for the patients. Often during the night, a bell rang and called him to a patient: sometimes it was an elegant carriage waiting, more often it was the ordinary peasant's cart taking him to the village, from which – after a few hours – he would come back with a basket of eggs as his honorarium. I met many people from many walks of life who knew him and respected him, but as far as friends were concerned, I don't think he had any. The point was perhaps, that his quixotry consisted in his ambition to translate those nineteenth century high principles not only into rhetorics, but also into the realities of everyday life – which wasn't an easy thing to do. I think, as a matter of fact, he was rather lonely. My brother Roman, after matriculating in our gymnasium, went to the front in 1920, from which he returned with a damaged spine (TB) and never recovered. He studied medicine as well, and died in 1929, immediately after receiving his diploma. My father died a year later, 1 March 1930. He was 58. I am today twenty years older and see him as somebody much younger than I am. All the same, a son's eye is of no importance; that's his business. But what colours will that life gain in the eyes of the historian, who will try to piece together little bits of the mosaic in order to replicate a small part of times past?

II. THE RINGS ON YOUR FINGERS

I was born ferocious. The first thing I did on this earth was to bite my mother's breast so badly that she had to be taken to Warsaw for hospital treatment. Thus I was given a wet-nurse.

Her name was . . . , I thought I knew, but now, when I have to put pen to paper, I see that I don't remember, not really: it was something like Kozłowska?, Kwiatkowska? Franciszka Kowalska? Well, it doesn't matter, does it? Years later, my mother would say 'the boy doesn't care about his wet-nurse at all', and I wondered, 'why should I care so especially for that *old* woman, who lived with the caretakers in the basement of these apartments?' I left Płock when I was 4, came back four years later, in 1918, after the Revolution: I didn't remember the place. And it is only now, in 1988, I realize that she couldn't have been as old as I thought she was, and that to be a wet-nurse, she must have had her own child. And so I must have somewhere in the world a little foster-brother or foster-sister, who will be some 79 years of age, assuming they are still alive.

I had another glimpse of that basement, thanks to still another war. The first war, Russia versus Japan, was the war of my father. He brought back from it his Order of St Stanislas and a little green kimono for my brother. The next war, the First World War, was the whole family's war. As the front moved eastwards, we moved from Płock, to Wilno, to Warsaw, to St Petersburg (Leningrad), to Wielkie Łuki, to Wilno, to Warsaw, and back to Płock on the Vistula. The Second World War was my war (*drôle de guerre*) . . . but there was still another war between the First World War and the Second. The war of 1920. It was my brother's war. I do remember him coming back from the front line (Lida?), shouting, 'nobody touch me! Must have a bath first. I'm covered in lice.' We could see the lice, but he wasn't killed in action and we couldn't see his spinal column, which became the cause of his death ten years later.

In 1920, Poland's independence only two years old, Piłsudski (with the notorious Petlura) went on his chestnut mare as far as Kiev (see *The Mystery of the Sardine,* p. 118), and then quickly back again to the very border of the Vistula. That is how, at the age of 10, I got in personal touch with the Soviet invader and had another experience of visiting the basement. A day or two before, I was helping to dig trenches at the approaches to the town from the east, and now I expected to go fighting there. Instead, I was sent to the basement, as it was considered that I'd be more safe there, thanks to the proletarian surroundings.

The first thing I saw there, through the very small, street-level window, was a man in a bearskin hat (the irony of it was that a similar bearskin was in our big bourgeois wardrobe, its small blue crown with a cross of silver ribbon on top – I didn't know and I still don't know, did it belong to my father or to his batman?). In his left fist the man was holding a handful of the black hair of Mrs Krukowa, a neighbour, now bent down. In his right hand was a knout with which he was whipping her stooping back. What puzzles me is that I don't remember having any sort of reaction. Not even as much as I would have when looking at a drawing. I just don't remember. Perhaps I hadn't had any, full stop.

The next thing I remember is the same bearskinned soldier (Cossack?), the same or not the same, coming to the basement, which was decorated with some big holy pictures hanging on the walls. The bearskinned soldier stood there facing me. 'Gold?' he asked. 'No', I shook my head. 'Show me your hands, boy', he said. I did, spreading my fingers. 'Ach', he said, disappointed. There were no rings on my fingers and no diamond bracelets on my wrists.

III. 'OH GOD!'
(For David Wiggins, a present to help him see the other side)

Catholics, Protestants, Jews, Mohammedans, Communists, Oh God! How thankful I am that I have never received any religious instruction. The first Bible that I saw was the one I bought in 1938 from a Salvation Army officer peddling his wares in a naughty *boîte* in Paris. It was lost in the war.

Today I have four and a half copies: one in English, one in French, one in Polish, one and a half in the modern English – an abomination committed by some who hate to admit that it was STYLE that had enobled what is in it.

We are all of us guests on this planet, and with guests – you know how it is. Some are nice, and some are tiresome, and some behave as if they were hosts, and even as they die, they believe that they have owned this planet, and the sun, and the air, and the history that took place before they were even born.

Russell said that he doesn't believe in God, but he finds the expression 'Oh God!' useful. On another occasion he said that the fact that one can name Something doesn't mean that that Something must necessarily exist. Yes, the existence of that Something is not necessarily a fact. But the fact that people *need* this very Something to exist and be named – that *is* a fact.

Whatever we shall call this Something – It, Him, Her – we shall soon find that it consists of two Enigmas. The Enigma of Creation and the Enigma of Behaviour.

The Enigma of Creation. It started in St Petersburg, and so I must have been four or six. I suppose I was a nice-looking little boy, as a young nice-looking lady, our neighbour, used to 'borrow' me to take me with her when going to a posh café where the presence of a child, like that of a puppy, might help to lure some handsome officers. The results of the innocent flirtations could have been a big box of chocolates. Once I was holding in both hands such a big box of chocolates, But I wasn't interested in the contents of the box, I was interested in the lid. Because on it, there was a picture of a pretty lady who was holding in her hands a box of chocolates on the lid of which there was a picture of a pretty lady holding in her hands a miniature box of chocolates on the lid of which . . . My eyes could not come any closer, my seeing processes could not go any further, but my thinking processes *could.* Now, if I came to the conclusion that there was no end to the series of pretty ladies holding boxes of chocolates – maybe, one day, I would become an axiomatic mathematician, or a dogmatic politician? On the other hand, if I thought that there must necessarily be somewhere there the very tiniest, ultimate, pretty lady whom you couldn't reduce any further, maybe I'd become a physicist, or a novelist . . .?

But time flies, I'm no longer four or six, I'm now ten or eleven, back in my native town, Płock. There I am, looking up and noticing above the cathedral portal a bronze, semi-circular high relief, in the middle of which sits the Holy Mother of the Enigma's son, holding in her hands the model of the whole cathedral, above the portal of which sits the . . . Now, this time I don't try to look 'within'. This time my mind works outwards and it makes me imagine a huge, no-longer-visible Mother of the Enigma's son holding in her hands the *real* cathedral, and then a bigger still, bigger than the sky, Mother of . . . There I stop. Either my intuition has told me that the whole thing is becoming ridiculous in the way that only grown-ups can appreciate, or else, perhaps . . . who can know? Perhaps the very biggest, the ultimate Mother, by some conjuring trick, a hocus-pocus which only grown-ups can explain, *is* the same person as the tiniest pretty lady with the box of chocolates?

Many years later, a few thousand copies of *Nature* glanced at, the old man finds now that scientists have become rather good at bringing little boys' *meta*-physical speculations into their physics. Their Big Bang back to the Genesis, their Catastrophes to the old Chaos, their one-thing-in-two-places-at-the-same-time, Wheeler, anthropic physics etc., back to Berkeley and the logical trick of his vanishing tree, delightfully encapsulated in this rhymed verse (and its response?):

> There was a young man who said 'God
> must think it exceedingly odd
> if he finds that this tree

continues to be
when there's no-one about in the Quad.'
(Monsignor Ronald Knox)

'Dear Sir, Your astonishment's odd,
I am always about in the Quad
And that's why the tree
will continue to be,
since observed by yours faithfully, God.'
(Anon)

And so I abandon the Enigma of the Creation, leaving both its physics and metaphysics in the hands of the scientists, and tried to concentrate on its twin God, The Enigma of Behaviour.

When talking of the Enigma of Behaviour, I need a special word to help me say what I want to say, and I can't find it in English, in Polish, in French, and I suspect it doesn't exist in any other language. That is why I limp around from one to another of those overlapping substitutes: decency, gentleness, the mystery of the body and the chemistry of the body [see *Hobson's Island*], duty, reciprocity, concern for others, love – most of them belonging rather to the post-natal than the pre-natal Enigmas.

Things seem to be done either from the Outside, like Michelangelo's *Pietà*, or the Inside, like God's egg or rose. If we go from *Pietà* to its Origin, we shall see a block of white marble, Michelangelo's tools, and – finally – Michelangelo's mind. If we go from Michelangelo's Mind to its Origin, we'll be led Inwards and, as it was the case of the egg and the rose, find ourselves on the way to *Infinite Regress* (Ryle).

I have an egg for breakfast, I admire a rose, but I am shattered by the *Pietà*.

I still haven't found a good word for that Something that does exist. Something without which our survival as a species would not be possible. Something biological, pre-natal, and so common that we tend to forget its very existence, namely – the fact that the untrained untaught animals take care of their children. The fact, simple in the forests, becomes enormously complicated with the growth of civilization.

And I still would like to know how much can be said on the subject without using such words as 'ought', etc., in front of the cart, or such terms as 'mathematical altruism' at the back of the horse. Perhaps the time will come when a novelist will have more to say on the subject than a 'computer-scientist'.

We have many words referring to viciousness. One of them is 'the Original Sin'. Perhaps its mirror image, the Original Virtue, would be that Something from which our study of the problems of humanity could start.

IV. A FLUORESCENT BOX OF TRICKS
(For Nick Wadley)

At school, gymnastics, ropes, vaulting horses, wall bars up to the ceiling. Hearing a faint crunching sound. At home, father said: 'collar bone', and took me to the hospital to have it X-rayed.

In those days an X-ray machine was not a lion or a tiger enclosed by heavy masses of metal, and let out for no longer than a fraction of a second, not to give you an overdose of radiation. It was a friendly lamb, a beautiful glass vacuum tube, sitting behind the shoulders murmuring. In front of you, touching your neck and body, was a fluorescent sheet of glass, about twenty-four inches square, framed like a picture, which the doctor held in his hands, looking at the black and grey shapes on the fluorescent background. By squeezing my head to the right, I could see a little of it beneath my chin. The doctor must have diagnosed that no great damage had been done, no need to immortalize the picture on a photographic plate. But I asked them to let me see more. They did. The enormous dose of radiation must have been the price paid for what, for me, was the First Photogram in Motion I had ever seen.

I wouldn't, of course, use (or perhaps I would, I don't remember) such words as *Art* and *Science* at the time, but that's what it was. X-rays emanating from the cathode, and the fluorescent rectangle showing shapes. Shapes showing a bit of nature as seen by a strange newly acquired way of seeing. There must be many ways of seeing. Some discover some bits of nature, and we call them science. Some create pictures that didn't exist before, and we call them Art. Some are like my X-ray picture, and it is difficult to distinguish which is which. It depends on the viewer how to classify them. It depends upon me! What an excitement for a young boy to feel all that, without even trying to put all this into words.

I couldn't put it into words, but I did *do* something, didn't I? I promised myself that when I am grown up I'll have my own beautiful Roentgen tube. At the time, the world of radiation was, of course, closed to me. But the world of photography, more easy to handle, was widely open.

Before the war (1914), we must have been better off than after (1918). My brother was no longer interested in the 'old junk' when we came back to our native town, Płock on the Vistula. But I found in it a strange object. A camera. Kodak. Must have been manufactured about the time I was born. 'What's in it?' I asked. 'Nothing.' 'How do you mean, nothing? There must be something. What is it?' 'Nothing, I told you. Nothing. Void. Open it.' I opened it. Between the lens at the front of the camera and the plate holder at the back – was nothing. Void. Into that void entered *snap = pstryk* onomatopoeia, the photography of today.

Snap is English. *Pstryk* is Polish. *Snap* has invaded all rich countries. People in poor countries dream of having a good *pstryk*. *Pstryks* and *snaps* must be good. They are good. Nowadays they can do everything that you, as an attachment to the camera, can do. *They* are the authors. They, the camera-makers, know best what is needed. If you don't comply with their wishes, you are at war. They teach the public to like what they – the monsters – think photographs should be. They had taken from the photography of the twenties its freedom.

Freedom of the twenties! Hocus-pocus, what started as freedom metamorphosed itself into the glory of advertising.

In 1920 I knew nothing of what was going on in photography, everything was so simple and easy, the most interesting part was not the camera, it was the 'laboratory'. Those pictures that were so-to-speak 'painted' directly by means of light, some people in Paris (or was it Berlin?) called (I learned that much later) 'photograms'.

[unfinished]

STORIES

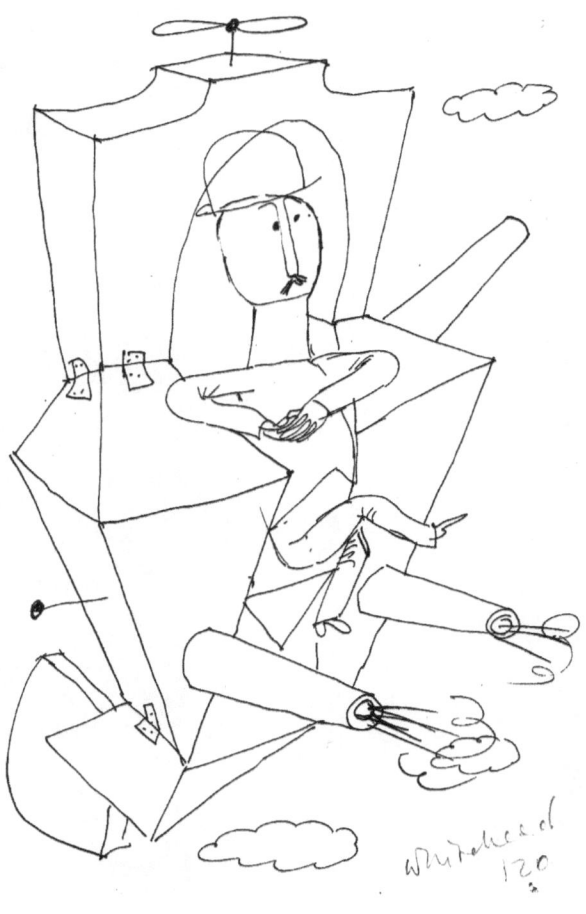

CRITICS AND MY TALKING DOG

Brutus is my dog. Three years ago, when he was a little puppy, it occurred to me that my difficulty in communicating with him derived not from his being less intelligent – he was not – but from the fact that the best part of my brain was connected to my eyes, while the best part of his brain was connected to his nose. The bit of brain dogs receive their visual patterns with is nothing better than a piece of cheddar. And so is the bit of brain we receive odourous patterns with. In short, I came to the conclusion that if we could so to speak *see* what dogs smell, or if they could so to speak *smell* what we see, it would result in a better understanding between our two species.

I decided to do something about it. Under local anaesthetic I opened the dog's skull, I severed the cords going from his eyes and his nose to his brain, and then I connected those going from his nose to those leading to the poor, optical part of his brain, while those going from his eyes I joined to those leading to the highly developed olfactory part of it. I say I connected or joined them, but you understand that I didn't do it by means of a soldering iron. The method I developed, aided all the time by the advice and help of my friend, Dr C.N. Smyth, has been described elsewhere, and the description is too technical to be repeated here. Suffice it to say that two capsules filled with organic semi-conductors had been prepared beforehand, and it was in these two capsules that the terminals of the cords were summarily embedded. I had my reasons to expect that the cut-off ends would, on their own initiative – so to speak –, build for themselves new paths through the semi-conductors. They did. Three weeks later, Brutus, with two capsules in his head, was as healthy and gay as ever. Three months later, he learned to read. His nose was not at all good for smelling. He used its wet black tip for turning the pages. After three months more (mark the sequence), he learned to talk. And now, finally, I have somebody to talk freely to.

I spend most of my time in my room with him, and that is why you don't see me very often in the public houses of Soho, drinking beer and convincing myself what a bright and angry old man I am. For hours I lie on my couch, looking up on to the sloping ceiling, while Brutus trails through the undergrowth of books and papers strewn in several layers on the floor – and sniffs. I said: sniffs. But it is with his *eyes* that he stiffs now.

He is a voracious reader. But I have never seen him read anything from beginning to end. His eyes constantly searching, he moves from one book to another, puts his nose between the pages, jumps back, jumps sideways, jumps forward, and every few minutes runs to me as if bringing a game bird, lays his head on the couch and says:

'Look, what does it all mean? Chardin says one doesn't paint with colours, one paints with emotions, Braque says that what distinguishes his and Picasso's cubist painting from that of their followers, is poetry. And then Rilke says that one doesn't write poetry with emotions, one writes it with experiences.'

'Quite so', I say, looking at the ceiling.

'But don't you see?' he insists. 'If, according to Braque, *their* pictures have poetry in them, then, according to Rilke, they are not painted with emotions. Yet, if they are not painted with emotions, then, according to Chardin, they are not pictures!... Because – because if they are pictures, then – according to Chardin – they have been painted with emotions, but if so then – according to Rilke – there is no poetry in them. But didn't Braque say that it was poetry that...'

'Take it easy, Brutus', I say, patting his lovely head. 'Don't get so excited!' I know, of course, that his life is shorter than ours, and so he has to squeeze things into more compactly. I know also that he can do this all right without special effort, as his breathing and heartbeat and capacity for learning is much quicker than ours, so it is all right, and there is no cause for anxiety. Nevertheless, at moments like this, I feel as if I was responsible for an abnormal, feverish child, and I try to calm him down as much as I can.

'Don't get so excited about their bloody words!' I repeat. 'Take it easy. Even the best painter is capable talking intellectual hot air when he tries to say something about art.'

'But what they say is a contradiction.' (He is so firmly convinced that he almost barks.)

'So what if it is?' I say lightly. I feel I shouldn't get involved in his worries. I feel he needs me like that, slightly aloof, lying here on the couch, motionless, unperturbed, firm – the couch being some sort of rock on to which he can always rest his forelegs when he feels like reporting one of his novel, exciting findings, or lay his head when it starts to whirl among the toxic specimens of that Garden of Letters which has so unexpectedly surrounded him with its odours. Yet he is obstinate:

'It is a contradiction', he repeats. 'Contradictions should not be allowed', he says. 'It is amoral to let them be', he adds. And there he is again, running from one corner to another, circling, ferreting among the volumes covered with dust. I know where they all are, and I don't even need to turn my head to see what he is reading. I bet he is looking for the definition of the word 'contradiction', as with his black muzzle he turns the pages of the dictionary. Yes, he is. He must have found the word 'paradox' there. And that leads him to Zeno, of course. Good heavens, how quick he is! How did he unearth that old copy of *MIND* with a paper on Achilles and the Tortoise? He wags his tail angrily. With contempt. They say dogs don't wag their tails when they are angry. So perhaps he does it sarcastically. But the copy of *MIND* is already forgotten. He's now trying with his teeth the quality of Allen & Unwin's cloth binding. It's a Russell. He's ferreting in the Index. Oh dear, he's not yet four years old and he's reading Russell's Theory of Description.

He lifts one ear and glances at me, somewhat suspiciously:
'Is it very wrong to ask, What is Art? ?'

'I don't know.'

'Shouldn't one rather ask: How do pictures actually Behave? ?'

'They hang', I answer. But I can see that he is above my flippancy.

'If they hang they must exist. One must exist in order to be able to hang. Unless one is a Golden Mountain, a Unicorn, or a Jew. But what else do they do? Can you describe it? If you could describe all pictures, we could find what the descriptions have in common, and that would be the answer to the question: "What is Art?" Or rather: "What is the meaning of the word ART as we use it?"'

'There is some barley water in the bowl in the corner', I say. He goes to the corner and starts to lap with his long pink tongue. But I see that he isn't to be drawn off his track.

'Do you know any descriptions of pictures?' (he asks).

'Well', I say, 'let me see . . .'

'Where?' (he insists).

I point to the bookshelf. To a volume of Diderot. He's looking at me reproachfully, saying nothing. The shelf is too high for him. I get off my couch – to take the book from the shelf – throw it on the floor for him and say:

'Listen Brutus. 200 years ago, in 1764, a man called Grimm asked a man called Denis Diderot to write some art criticism for him. Well, here it is. You will find it on the pages headed *SALONS*. When Grimm read them, he exclaimed:

> J'en jure sur mon âme,
> aucun homme n'a fait et ne fera
> pareille chose.'[1]

And I go back on to my couch.
Brutus's nose is already in the book. *SALONS* by Diderot. The ice cream van, somewhere in the street, plays that horrid electronic tune which will go on till a lascivious infant stops the van to buy his

1   Upon my soul, no man has ever done or will ever do anything like that!

orgiastic ice cream; then the tune will stop too, in the middle of the bar, to start again from the middle of the same bar. If the blind beggar on the corner by the chemists's played his gramophone record half as loudly, the policewoman there would have arrested him a long time ago. That's what I think. And it is a revolutionary thought, I think. And it isn't done to have revolutionary thoughts in England. It classifies you to your disadvantage. Because there is a difference between the two cases: the blind man functions as a beggar, while the ice cream man functions as a respectable salesman, a sort of Old Bond Street Art Dealer, so I should be ashamed of myself – all right, I shall, but let the van stop playing that tune! That's better, it must have turned the corner. I'm sure it didn't disturb Brutus. He lifts his head, well . . . what is it?

'He's wrong!'

'Who?' (I ask).

'Grimm.'

'Why?'

'Because he said nobody would ever write anything like SALONS, and I have that persistent, toothachey feeling that something of the kind is going on all the time . . .'

'Brutus,' I interrupted him. 'Do you realise that you've never had toothache? How can you know what a toothachey feeling is?'

'I have observed your toothache,' (he answered). 'Don't you remember, last year, before you decided to go to the dentist? The behaviour of your body then was itself a description of your ache, and, by watching it, I was, so to speak, reading that description. Now, you know that even when one reads silently, there is still some movement going on in one's muscles and larynx and . . .'

'I didn't know you'd read Watson,' I say.

'I haven't,' (he answers).

'All right,' I say. 'Never mind. So you were spying on me when I had a toothache, and . . .'

'. . . and the muscles of my body were repeating all the movements of the muscles of your body. To a very minute degree, of course. A kind of miniature replica of what your body was describing to me. And once that replica was in me, I felt exactly what that something in my tooth would have to be, to be able to create the same kind of description. Though stronger. And here I think that all philosophers I read in your books are wrong when they think that the ache they experience is the thing they can be most certain of. It is not so. It is the pregnant female (of your species or of mine) who forgets her pains as soon as she is all right again. The obstetrician does not forget her pains. Because he remembers the description. And so it is with your toothache. You have nine tenths of your ache, and you were too busy to memorise the movements your body was performing at the time. But I observed them at leisure. I can repeat the miniature replica of them any time. And so I conclude that at this moment I know better what toothache is than you do. Therefore, I am perfectly well entitled to use the expression: a toothachey feeling that something of the kind is going on all the time.'

'What's going on all the time?'

'Writing. Writing in the fashion of Diderot's, in *SALONS.*'

'My dear Brutus! That is simply impossible. Just look at modern painting and you will see that one couldn't. Even if one wanted to. And nobody does. Neither Eric Newton nor John Berger.'

'I know.'

'Well then . . .'

'And nevertheless I am quite sure that I read something very like that, – all the time.'

'Where?'

'Where?' he repeats. He tucks up his tail and looks worried. Very worried indeed. He jerks his head back, sinks his muzzle into the fur on his spine and starts to gnaw it.

'Brutus! Don't tell me you've got a flea!'

But he is already under one of my two tables. A booty of a dozen newspapers and weeklies in his mouth, he comes back. Throws them on my couch. And . . . well?

'Of course I was right. They *do* write criticism like that today. Only it is not about painting. It is about films.'

We spent several hours looking through the review pages of the newspapers and, at the same time, through the old, yellowed with age, pages of SALONS.

'You hold the book,' (he said). 'It's easier for you. You've got what you call "hands". And I'll sit on the newsprint.'

So we did. And now he reads from a film review, and I follow him from SALONS. Quote after quote. Bite and bite.
Aloud:

'The ruined city of Timgad rises majestically from the desert . . .'
Thus Brutus, from a film review.
And now I, from Diderot's SALONS:
'O les belles, les sublimes ruines! Quelle fermeté, et en meme temps quelle légèreté, sûreté, facilité de pinceau; Quel effet! quelle grandeur! quelle noblesse!'[2]

'. . . the fluted columns of white limestone soar upwards into the blue oblivion of the sky . . .'

'L'étonnante dégradation de lumière! comme elle s'affaiblit en descendant du haut de cette voûte, sur la longueur de ces colonnes!'[3]

And now he again, from his film reviews:
'And the Trajan arch frowns down upon the absurdities of modern man.'

And I, from my Diderot:
'Avec quell étonnement, quelle surprise je regarde cette voûte brisée,

2 "O beautiful, O sublime ruins! How vigorous, and at the same time how light, how sure, how fluent his brush! How effective! how imposing! how noble!"
3 "What astonishing graduation in the light! How it declines as it descends from the top of that arch down the length of those columns!"

les masses surimposées à cette voûte! Les peuples qui ont élevé ce monument, où sont-ils? que sont-ils devenus?' [4]

'The film is in colour, and those magnificent glimpses of the grandeur that was Rome almost justify the futility of the story.'

'Rien, dans un tableau, n'appelle comme la couleur vraie; elle parle à l'ignorant comme au savant. Un demiconnaisseur passera sans s'arrêter devant un chef-d'oeuvre de dessin, d'expression, de composition; l'oeil n'a jamais négligé la coloriste . . . C'est un effet merveilleux produit sans efforts. On ne songe pas à l'art. On admire, et c'est de l'admiration meme que l'on accorde à la nature.' [5]

'Your turn, Brutus.'

'All right. This is from a Sunday paper: "I can see no point in beating about the burning bush. To me The Ten Commandments seems a long, dull, vulgar, meretricious, mediocre picture . . ."'

'C'est pis que jamais. Autre logogriphe plus froid, plus impertinent, plus obscure encore que les precedents.' [6]

'I won't go so far as to say that it is bogus, because I believe Cecil B. de Mille, whose darling project it is, to have been quite sincere in his intentions. I think he really meant to strike a blow for truth, to fill his audience with spiritual grace, to send them away from the theatre

---

4   "With what astonishment, with what surprise do I regard that shattered arch, the masses superimposed on that arch! Where are they, the peoples who elevated that monument? What has happened to them?"

5   "Nothing in a painting is as appealing as true colour; it speaks to the ignoramus and the scholar alike. The amateur will not stop to look at a masterpiece of drawing, expression, or composition, but his eyes will always be caught by the colourist... It is a marvellous effect, produced without effort. We do not think about art. We admire, and it is the same admiration that we feel for nature." [BW]

6   "It is worse than ever. Another logogriph even colder, more impertinent, more obscure than its predecessors."

in some way uplifted and improved. It is just unfortunate that he has a limited imagination . . .'

'Eh bien, mon ami, y avez-vous jamais rien compris? Ça, mettez voyre esprit à la torture, et dites-moi le sens qu'il y a là dedans. Je gage que La Grenée n'en sait pas là-dessus plus que nous. Et puis, qui s'est jamais avisé de montrer la Religion, la Verité, la Justice, les êtres les plus venerable, les êtres du monde les plus anciens, sous des symbols aussi puérils? De bonne foi, sont-ce là leur caractère, leur expression?'[7]

'Let me finish my quotation: "It is just unfortunate that he has a limited imagination, is accustomed to work with a dollar index, and can think aloud only in clichés." Now let me hear your Diderot.'

'Mais, me répond l'artiste, vous ne savez pas que ces vertus sont des dessus de porte pour un receveur général des finances? Je haue les épaules, et je me tais, après avoir dit à M. La Grenée un petit mot sur le genre allégorique.'[8]

'Your Diderot is much more long-winded than my reviewer.'
'Yes, he is. In his day, printing was set by hand. So one had plenty of time. Now we use setting machines. So we have to hurry. Time is precious. Amortisation. You can call it: The Paradox of the Printer.

7 "Well, my friend, have you ever been able to make anything of such stuff? Come, rack your brains, and tell me what meaning it has. I wager La Grenée knows it no more than we do. Moreover, who ever took it into his head to show Religion, Truth, Justice, the most venerable things, the most ancient things in the world, by means of such puerile symbols? In all good faith, is *that* their character, is *that* their expression?"
8 "'But,' the artist replies, 'Don't you realize that a tax collector would regard these virtues as little more than luxuries for the leisured class?' I shrug my shoulders and keep quiet, after having said a word or two about the allegorical genre to M. La Grenée." [BW]

Well, but that's enough.'

'How do you mean: enough?'

'I said: enough!'

'Oh, but please read his *L'Accordée de Village* by Greuze. He describes everything there, even the sound track: "*Jeanette est douce et sage; elle fera ton bonheur; songe à faire le sien . . .*"[9] You will see, it is like a scenario from the "Free Cinema" they show in the National Film Theatre. Lorenza Mazetti, you know, and Paolozzi as Jean, *"un brave garçon, honnête et laborieux".*[10]

'We'll read it tomorrow, Brutus.'

'But look, just look at the titles of the pictures in his *SALONS*. They read exactly like a sequence from a film script:

     1. Un commencement d'orage au soleil couchant

     2. Une tempête

     3. Un naufrage

     4. Le fils ingrate

     5. Une tête de fille

     6. L'amour menaçant

     7. Jeune fille qui envoie un baiser

     8. La mère bienaimée

     9. Un autre naufrage

     10. Le mauvais fils puni

     11. La jeune fille pleure son oiseau mort

     12. Trois paysages sous un meme numéro

9   *The Village Bride.* "Jeanette is sweet and pure; she will make you happy; try to make her happy, too . . ."
10 "a worthy fellow, honest and industrious".

13. Le coucher de la mariée

14. Une matinée après la pluie...' [11]

'Stop it, Brutus!' 'But you don't see the point! But you don't see the point! Woof! Woof! Woof!' (he barks, and I don't like to see him so excited). 'The point is that the INTERPRETATION ACT, 1889, passed in Parliament that year, outflanked Aristotle long before Bertie Russell did.'

'Brutus! Behave yourself!'

'All right. But listen. In the INTERPRETATION ACT, 1889, Parliament that *"he"* will also mean *"she"* if the person talked about is a female, and that the *singular* will also mean the *plural* and vice versa, which breaks the most fundamental assumptions of Aristotelian philosophy, but is all right if you think that Existence should be asserted only of Description, – and in 1932, the High Court decided that *"road"* includes the *foot-way* as well as the *carriage-way;* and you know that while for the purpose of spending money a wife's earnings are *her* income, for the purpose of the Income Tax Inspector your wife's earnings are *your* income; – Thus, for the purpose of the Frame-Maker and the Colour-Merchant, Greuze and Girodet and Gros belong to the same catergory as Picasso and Braque and Nicholson and Bacon; – But if you happen to think that Existence should be asserted only of Descriptions, then the analysis of the Descriptions produced by Diderot, and by the Film Reviewers will force you to conclude that XVIIIth century French painting belongs in the same catergory as XXth century Film and Glorious Technicolor. I mean that their paintings were for the public not what your paintings are for

11   1. The beginning of a storm at sunset; 2. A tempest; 3. A shipwreck; 4. The ungrateful son; 5. Head of a girl; 6. The threatening love; 7. Girl who sends a kiss; 8. The beloved mother; 9. Another shipwreck; 10. The wicked son punished; 11. The girl weeps for her dead bird; 12. Three landscapes with the same number; 13. The bride's bedtime; 14. Morning after rain.

you, but what films are for you. While modern painting beginning, let's say, with Seurat . . .'

'For heaven's sake, Brutus, stop it.' (I command) 'You are quite feverish!' But he doesn't listen to me.

'Have you read your Poincaré?' (he asks)

'I'll tell you tomorrow. Now calm down, and . . .'

'Well,' (he snarls), 'Poincaré said Mathematics is the art of giving the same name to different things.'

'You can tell me about it tomorrow.'

'But you see his meaning, don't you? He means that the same regularities occur in various places which used to be considered entirely different. Such places as rhe orbits of planets, the shells of snails, Harvey's Mathematical Models, and Henry Moore's or Barbara Hepworth's sculpture. And as mathematics is . . .'

'Leave it till tomorrow, Brutus, please,' I say. But he goes on:
'. . . and as mathematics is the study of all possible regularities that can be recognized by your – or my! – mind . . .'

'Brutus!' (I interrupt him). 'Look at your hindlegs!' He's frightfully excited. Barks impatiently, and says 'I can prove to you that both Cubism and Social Realism contain regularities that occur in the outward aspect of the new industrial landscape, and Pop-Art is the industrial townscape's sentimental, naive, naturalistic ANGELUS. I mean Jean-François Millet . . .'

'You will prove it to me tomorrow.'

'. . . while both Modrians and Action Painting contain regularities which occur in the mind of those chaps you call physicists, and . . .'

'Tomorrow!'

'You'll see, I'll bite out of *DISCOVERY,* or *NATURE,* or *The New Scientist,* some pictures and show them to you alongside some photographs from the West End art gallery catalogues, and you won't know which comes from where. And I can prove to you that the regularities the physicists are finding in Nature were first discovered by painters . . .'

'Shut up!'

'. . . and if the painters hadn't discovered them first, the physicists couldn't possibly have recognized them as regularities even if they were gaping at them through their telescopes and microscopes for bloody centuries!'

'Brutus!'

'And the nameless regularities painters are discovering today, scientists will be discovering tomorrow . . .'

I jumped off my couch.

'Brutus, that's enough! We shall go for a walk now.'

We climb down the stairs, – and now, as we come to the front door, he whispers:

'Listen!'

He is not allowed to talk in the street. Imagine the sensation it would create. Not so much among Englishmen as among other dogs. Hence it is agreed between us that if he has something to tell me he will do so before I open the front door. And so I bend nearer to him and say: 'Yes?'

'Listen,' (he repeats, in a very low voice) 'Do you remember the passage Diderot wrote about Boucher?

"Je ne sais que dire de cet homme-ci. La dégradation du goût, de la couleur, de la composition, des caractères, de l'expression, du dessin, a suivi pas à pas la dégradation des moeurs. Que voulez-vous que cet artiste jette sur la toile? ce qu'il a dans l'imagination; et que peut avoir dans l'imagination un homme qui passe sa vie avec les prostituées du plus bas état?"'[12]

'Well, Brutus. What about it?'

'Well . . . Can you tell me what is, exactly, *"une prostituée"*?'

'Well . . . I don't think I can tell you exactly. But approximately, it is a female who is a female as a profession.'

'A human female, or a canine female?'

'A human.'

12   "I don't know what to say about that fellow. The degradation of his taste, of his colour, of his composition, of his characters, of his expression, of his drawing, has followed, step by step, the degradation of his morals. What can such an artist throw upon his canvas? – What is in his imagination; and what can there be in the imagination of a man who spends his life with prostituées of the lowest type?"

'Well . . . And what about canine ones?'

'All right, Brutus.' (I say, opening the door). 'I'll think about it.'

The street is soot black and sodium-light yellow. Both the carriage-way and the foot-way. Bicycles and bipeds, quadricycles and quadrupeds, move along in the black and yellow darkness and display their applications of some few regularities in nature. I look at the base of a lamp-post, and realise that ever since his nose has got connected with the less developed part of his brain, Brutus is not able to tell a bitch from a dog until he *sees* her.

CASTOR & POLLUX

And so they went to the house of Bogalawd.

"I wish you were dead," said Bogalawd.

Pollux turned to Castor and asked:

"Ought we not to cut his head off?"

Castor directed a penetrating, searching look at Bogalawd's head for the purpose of examining it thoroughly and forming a judgment concerning it.

"Not worth it," he said. "Such a poor head. No more than two poor eyes, and one poor nose, and one poor mouth!"

"I wish you were dead," repeated Bogalawd.

"Why?" asked Pollux.

"You don't know what life is like. I mean here, in my house, all around; and below, in the basement."

"Many people?" asked Castor.

"Oh," answered Bogalawd, "many too many. They live as in hell."

"Cannot one help them?" asked Pollux.

"No," said Bogalawd. "Impossible. They are unhappy."

"Well?" asked Castor.

"Every single method applied in order to ease them will itself add to their unhappiness."

"tsapity," said Pollux.

Castor sighed and said:

"May we not stay here, in the hall, until the morning twilight, when the sky will be illuminated by the reflection of the rays of the rising sun on the clouds of dust, &c., suspended in the atmosphere, before it will rise above the horizon. May we not wait here until the dawn is clear, bright yellow, or for even a short time, until it is gold, or only until it is orange, or at least until it is a deep red. Could you not bring us a bed here?"

"I certainly could," said Bogalawd, "but there are not many beds down there. So they'll be even more unhappy if I take one away."

"Well," said Castor, "and could you not bring us a glass of water, for we are craving for something to drink."

"I certainly could," said Bogalawd, "but there are many there who experience thirst, who have a need of liquid in their systems; so if I take some water from them it will add to their unhappiness."

"Well," said Castor, "there is nothing for us to do here but to say good-bye and go straight away."

"You certainly can say good-bye and go straight away," said Bogalawd, "but the floor between the door and that part upon which you are now standing is rotten, and it screams when one puts one's foot upon it. And, below, there live women who have headaches, cerebrotonic men who write poetry, and nervous children who fear screech-owls. And the screeching produced by the rotten timber when you are going from here to the door will add to their unhappiness."

"Then what can we do?" asked Castor.

"Nothing!" said Bogalawd. "I said I wished you were dead."

"But if we die here, where we stand," said Pollux, "and what we are built of remains here, it will decompose and then there will be a smell which will add to their unhappiness."

"Oh, no!" said Bogalawd. "They like the smell of dead bodies decomposed by *natural* processes through exposure to air, moisture &c. The natural full-smelling decomposition of organic matter – that's what they like most of all; it will not add to their unhappiness."

"If that is so, pray kill us," said Castor.

"If that is so, pray kill us," said Pollux.

But Bogalawd said:

"I don't like to kill. If you want to be killed, you can yourselves kill yourselves."

"Is it feasible?" asked Castor.

"It isn't," said Pollux. "If *A* is doing something, and *B* comments on what *A* is doing, *B's* action is of a higher order than *A's* action. If *B* is killing *A*, killing is a higher order than living. And if *I* am killing *myself*, *I* belongs to a higher order than *myself*. Well, *I* can kill *myself*, but whom is going to kill *I*? And who is going to kill him who will kill *I*? And who is going to kill him who will kill him who will kill *I*? And who is going to kill him who will kill him who will kill him who . . ."

"Nonsense," said Bogalawd. "Modern philosophy is nonsense. You forget that you are double, and that Castor may kill Pollux and Pollux may kill Castor. I mean: at the same moment."

"Do you think so?" said Castor.

"Let us try," said Pollux.

So Pollux placed the point of his sword upon the breast of Castor, and Castor placed the point of his sword upon the breast of Pollux, and they thrust them simultaneously through their respective bodies.

And that is the true story about the end of the two brothers of Helen, the children of Leda. Amen.

HE WAS 47 OR 48

He was 47 or 48 and cried several times a day. His wife took him once to a psychologist but it didn't help him. It sufficed to utter a word about the hunger in China, about a train derailed in Australia, or about a cat drowned in a waste pit in Bayswater; it sufficed to lend him a historical book containing an account of somebody's suffering 2000 years ago, or a fantastic novel containing some account of somebody's suffering 2000 years ahead, – to make his lips tremble nervously, to make his mouth gulp air rapidly, and to make his eyes secrete an abundance of big full-sized tears.

Except for that he was a perfectly normal homo. His friends got used to his paroxysms of crying, or, at least, they pretended to, as it has been rather tiring, after all. But they did like him and there was always a touch of cordiality in their voice when they said: "What a sensitive fellow George is . . ." – even if they meant by 'sensitive' that there was something wrong in his grey cells. "What a sensitive fellow George is" they used to whisper, "if you cut your finger in his presence he'll be ready to die of grief".

But it wasn't true. It happened that I cut my finger in his presence. And to my astonishment he didn't cry at all. He took me into the bathroom, washed my hand under the tap, found a piece of elastoplast and made me a perfect dressing. And he looked very happy all this time, making jokes, his face radiant with joy.

I remembered that I saw already the same expression of joy once, when he threw a threepenny piece into the box of a man without legs and who, with his right hand, drew pictures on the pavement outside the National Gallery, and his wife told me that he didn't cry at all and was almost happy (she said 'almost' because she didn't dare to say just plain 'happy') when he had to go with a cup of tea to their neighbours, a widow, and announce to her that her child had been killed by a car near the corner of Notting Hill Gate and Church Street. But, nevertheless, when his eye caught in the evening paper a note prophecying that in the next year there will be such and such a number of street casualties – his lips started to tremble, his mouth gasped for air, and his eyes started to weep.

"Perhaps you shouldn't stop visiting the psychologist . . ." said his wife mournfully.

"No," he answered, after drying his eyes with his palm. "I don't think he could help me. In any case that cure has to take about three years. And if you count his fees it will make some £600. And if I have £600, which I have not, I would prefer to retire for a year and we could spend a whole year somewhere on the seaside."

"Oh, George!" said his wife, "but if we were on the seaside you'll have to see sometimes a poor jelly-fish drying on the sand; wouldn't that make you cry?"

"No, it wouldn't".

Then I decided to take part in that talk. Like all his friends, I was used to his crying over any trifle, and what I had been asking myself for a long time wasn't why he was crying, but why sometimes he wasn't. Why he wasn't crying when I cut my finger, when he saw a man without legs and the right hand, when the child was killed by a car. And why he thinks now that he will not cry when he'll see a jelly-fish drying on the sand.

"Why?" I said.

"You see . . ." he said, "I shall put it back into the sea. I am not crying when I can help a little, when I can do something, when I can act.

I'm crying only when I'm powerless."

"Look, George!" I said, and it was perhaps very silly of me to say what I said – "You know there are plenty of jelly-fishes on the sea-side. You'll have a full-time lunatic job there to throw them all back into the sea. You'll not be able to do it, my friend."

He glanced at me inquisitively and I felt that his imagination showed him a picture of an army of poor jelly-fishes drying in the sun, and I saw that his lips started to shake with rapid intermittent movements . . .

"Stop that, George!" I shouted with anger, "You megalomaniac!"

It was the last word he could expect to be directed to him. He was sure there was not a trace of megalomania in him, and that nobody ever could suppose such an absurd and unjust thing. He looked at me as if I became crazy. But, and I don't know why, I was really very angry. "What do you think you are? I asked, "God, The Creator Almighty?! Is it you who created life as it is, and all things as they are? You fool, do you mean that you are responsible for everything that happens? You see yourself as almighty enough to prevent all jelly-fishes from being dehydrated by the sun?!"

I said all that, and went out.

I have never seen him since, during my nights. And I believe I never said that I saw him in the daytime.

CHAPTER 18

'Oh, piss off,' Judith said and put the receiver down.

On the road to Damascus a jet-black poodle snuffled his way along. His track was traced with little tongues of fire, though that might have been some optical illusion. And the little squeals of pain uttered by the little tongues of fire might have been some acoustical illusion. But the jet-black poodle-dog was not an illusion.

And it was the middle of the day, and a light came from the sky, more brilliant than the sun, and a white poodle appeared on the road in front of the black poodle and said: 'Poodle, Poodle, why do you persecute me?' And the Black Poodle said: 'Why are you always telling me that? You know very well that I'm only doing my job.'

'That's what *you* say,' said the White Poodle.

'That's what *He* ordained,' said the Black Poodle. 'You select-in, and I select-out. Continuous Creation.'

'Of what?' asked the White Poodle.

'Of men,' the Black Poodle answered.

'But do not men exist already?' exclaimed the White Poodle. 'Have I not suffered for them?"

The Black Poodle snuffled at him confidently, almost as if they were old friends. Then he settled on his hocks and said:

'Yes, you have. But were they men? In a series of forms graduating insensibly from some ape-like creature to man as he will exist in the future, it would be impossible to fix on any definite point where the term "man" ought to be used.'

'Quoting?' asked the White Poodle.

'Not literally,' said the Black Poodle.

Now the White Poodle became whiter still and commanded:

'Rise to your hind feet and stand upright!' And when the Black Poodle did so, he said: 'Bow!' And when the Black Poodle did so, he asked sternly: "Where have you been?"

'I have been attending a flower,' said the Black Poodle.

The whiteness of the White Poodle softened.

'Well, now,' he said. 'Lie at my feet and tell me all about it. What sort of flower was it?'

'A flower-pot flower,' said the Black Poodle. 'It was a pretty flower-pot flower in a flower-pot, but it thought the flower-pot it was in was everything that there was, that it was the whole world, and as the flower-pot was rather small and cramp, the flower thought that the whole world is rather small and cramp, no room to swing a cat, very logical, don't you think?, so I thought it was a sin and a shame to leave it under that ignorant illusion, considering all the magnitude and power and glory of the universe, the visible and invisible, and so I thought of transplanting the flower into a bigger flower-pot, a commendable thought, don't you think?'

'And what did you do to achieve that?' asked the White Poodle.

'Well,' the Black Poodle said. 'To begin with, I hid in her wardrobe.'

'*Her* wardrobe?' asked the White Poodle.

'Yes,' said the Black Poodle. 'Didn't I tell you that the cramp flower-pot was female?'

'No, you didn't,' said the White Poodle.

'Well, she was,' said the Black Poodle.

There was a longish pause, and then the White Poodle fixed his eyes on the Black Poodle and asked:

'And who was that flower-woman, if you please?'

'She was not a flower-woman,' the Black Poodle answered. 'She was a school teacher.'

'And what was her name?'

'Oh!' the Black Poodle exclaimed. "What does a name matter? Think of the names they give *me*! Proud Spawn of hell! Destroyer! Prince of Flies! Tongue of Lies! And I'm not that at all, am I? I am Part of a power, you may call the part I am "evil", but the Whole of which I am part is good, don't you think? We are both just two bits of His evolutionary method. You select creatures in, I weed them out. If you were more careful eugenically, I would have less to weed out ethically.'

But the White Poodle seemed not to have been listening. 'What was her name?' he repeated.

'Mrs Judith Sheridan,' the Black Poodle murmured at length.

'Wife of Anthony Sheridan?'

'Well, now you know,' the Black Poodle said. 'And I hope you'll not try to win her to her harm, with your particular determinants of moral ideas. Yes, it was Mrs Sheridan, wife of Anthony, who had just lost his job on the *Chronicle*, and thought that was the end of the world, and she also though that was the end of the world, a holocaust of the flower-pot, ha ha, and so when he phoned her for the fourth time to tell her how happy he was to be free, she put the receiver down and said: "Oh piss off!"'

'Say it again,' the White Poodle asked, and his hind leg twitched.

'"Oh piss off!", she said and hung up. And the time was 8 o'clock on her watch, and ten past eight on his watch, because he had set his in the pub, and pub clocks are always ten minutes fast. And at that moment the door bell rang and there was a creature five foot ten inches, twelve stone, navy blue serge suit, and the creature said "Are you Mrs Anthony Sheridan?", and she said "Yes . . .?" and he said "I am Detective Sergeant Brown. May I come in?", and she showed him in her yellow brocaded chair, and he said "I understand, Mrs

Sheridan, that you are a sister of Miss Rachel Armstrong," and she jumped up and said "Oh how marvellous that you have come, Mr Brown. I have been wanting to go to the station but I couldn't leave Aaron alone with no babysitter. Have you brought Jolyon with you? You must bring Jolyon!" "And who is Jolyon?" he asked and took a notebook out of his pocket. "Jolyon is Rachel's little boy," she said and he wrote *Jolyon* in his notebook, and she said "And where is he, anyway? He can't spend the night at the police station. I want him here, he can sleep with Aaron." "And who is Aaron, Mrs Sheridan?" he asked, "Aaron is *my* little boy, he's asleep upstairs, that's why I couldn't leave him alone and . . ." He wrote *Aaron* in his notebook. She stood up. "Would you have a glass of sherry, Superintendent?" she asked. "It's very kind of you, Mrs Sheridan, but I don't think I will." "Well, I must have a glass of sherry" she said and poured two glasses. Then she took a sip and said "I am so glad you have come, Superintendent . . .", "*Sergeant* . . ." he corrected her. "Sorry" she said "but there is something else I want to ask you. You see, my two little girls went to the Hampstead fair this morning and they haven't come back yet. I know they are growing up, and they will be late more and more often, but this is the first time, and I don't know if I should be anxious or not. Can you tell me whether I should be anxious? It's already ten past eight. You see, Charlotte is twelve and Harriet is eleven." He nodded and wrote down *Charlotte 12* and *Harriet 11*. Then he turned to her and asked "Would you mind if I smoked, Mrs Sheridan?" "Oh, no, please do," she said, and he lit his pipe and asked "And how long have you known your sister?" "How do you mean: How long? I've known her since I was born." "And how old are you, if I may ask?" he asked and she said "Oh, I see what you mean. Well, I've known her since *she* was born," and then she added "But look here, what about Jolyon?, it's getting so late! Perhaps you could phone and ask that nice policewoman to bring Jolyon here?" "And when did you see her last?" he asked. "That policewoman with the pony tail? I think her name was Liz. I saw her when she brought Aaron home. About fiveish, I should say . . ." "No, no" he said, "I didn't mean Liz, I meant: When did you see your sister Rachel last?" and she said "Oh, I saw her today, of course. She came with Jolyon in the morning to take Aaron to the Hampstead fair," and he said "But I thought it was the girls who went to the fair," and she said "Oh, they went earlier. They went by tube, and they haven't come back yet, as I told you." "And how did Mrs Armstrong go?" he asked. "*Miss* Armstrong," she corrected him. "O yes, so it is, Miss Armstrong. And do you know Mr Armstrong, Mrs Sheridan?" "Which Mr Armstrong?" she asked. "The little boy's father, Aaron's father," he said, and she said "Good Lord, Aaron's father is "Anthony Sheridan, my husband," and he said "Oh yes, I meant the other little boy's father, Jolyon's father," and she said "Well, his father's name is not Mr Armstrong." "And what is his name, Mrs Sheridan?" "I don't know," she said. "You don't know?" "No." "Well, then, if I may ask, if you don't know his name how do you know that his name is not Armstrong?" "Oh really, Mr Brown," she said, "are these questions necessary? All I want is . . ." "I know, Mrs Sheridan, and I'm trying to help. Do you know any other of Miss Armstrong's friends? Her present gentlemen friends?" "No, I don't," she said and she felt awkward because she was still wearing the white trousers which belonged to Rachel's rich boyfriend. "No, I don't," she repeated, and he reached for his glass of sherry and said "This is not, strictly speaking, official, Mrs Sheridan, and you are under no obligation to answer my questions, under no obligation whatsoever, but it would be helpful if you did." "I *was* answering your questions," she said. "Well," he said, "I asked you a long time ago how she went, and you didn't answer me." "How who went where?" she asked. "Now, now, Mrs Armstrong," he said. "*Sheridan*," she corrected him. "Now, now, Mrs Sheridan," he repeated, "you told me that your daughters went to Hampstead by tube, and I asked you: And how did your sister go?, and you didn't answer." "Oh," she said, "Rachel has a car." "Yes, we know that she has a car, but did she go by car?" "She did." "How do you know?" "I watched from the door as she arranged the boys in the back seat of the brake, and off they went." "And you are sure it was her car, Mrs Sheridan?" "Yes, of course, it had some transfers on the bonnet." "And do you remember the time they left?" "Oh, I don't know, about half past nine, I should say." He sighed. "And that was the last time you saw her?" "Oh no," she cried out. "I saw her again just before lunch time." "You did *not* tell me that, Mrs Sheridan," he said drily. And then asked "Did you expect her to come back to lunch? "Well, not exactly," she said. "So it was unexpected?" "No, not exactly," she repeated. "But in sort of way?" he suggested. "Well, yes." "And did she come back by car?" "Presumably." "Why presumably? Didn't you see her coming?" "No, I was in the kitchen." "So the front door was open?" "No, you see, the boys came first, through the back door, the garden door, straight into the kitchen." "And how soon after them did she appear, Mrs Sheridan?" "A few minutes." "Minutes?" "Oh dear, it's because she was limping and asked to boys to run on. She went on the children's roundabout but the little wooden horse wasn't big enough for her and she fell off and hurt herself. So she came to bathe her knee, bound it up, and I lent her my tights." "And how do you know that she fell off the roundabout?" he asked. "Indeed," she exclaimed, "I saw her knee and I saw scratches on her face!" "Yes, but you didn't see the roundabout." "No." "So how do you know that she fell off?" "She told me herself. *And* the boys." "Aaron or Jolyon?" he asked. "Oh really, Mr Brown, does it really matter? I think it was Aaron. And Jolyon. Both." There was a brief silence. Then he leaned forward and said "Listen to me, Mrs Sheridan. If your sister didn't have a car, then how could she be at Hampstead in the morning, then – just before lunch time – here, and then, again – just before lunch time – at Trafalgar Square? On the other hand, if she did have a car, then what the hell was she doing on Platform One, Baker Street Station? At noon?" She gasped. "Then perhaps it wasn't Rachel at all?" she exclaimed hopefully. "Well," he said, "I don't know. But you see now how careful we must be. You said – just before lunch time – that's pretty vague. Could you be more precise? Did anybody see her when she came here with her bruised knee?" "Oh, Yes." "Who?" She hesitated for a moment. "Mr Walker was here. He saw Rachel coming." "And who is Mr Walker, please?" "Raffles Walker, a domestic. Sent by the agency." "On Easter Saturday?" he asked. She nodded. And then she looked at him and said, casually, "Oh, yes, and Mrs Twomey was here, we were all together in the kitchen." "And you were giving her lunch in the kitchen, Mrs Sheridan, if you don't mind my asking?" "No, no. Mrs Twomey didn't stay for lunch. She just came to see Mr Walker." "Indeed," he said. "You see Mr Walker is her lodger." "Now, let me put things straight, Mrs Sheridan. Mr Walker, a domestic, is a lodger of Mrs Twomey, and she came to see him in your kitchen?" "Oh, don't be a snob, Mr Brown. She brought him an urgent telegram." "Do you happen to know from whom?" "I think it was from his mother." He fixed his eyes on her and said "Are you quite certain it was Mrs Twomey?" "But of course," she said, "she is Mr Twomey's mother. He is the editor of the *Chronicle*. And my husband is a political journalist under his editorship." "Mr Raoul Twomey?" he asked. "Yes." He emptied his pipe slowly and said "Now, listen carefully, Mrs Sheridan. Do you recall . . . Did Mrs Twomey say anything about her son during your conversation in the kitchen?" "No, I don't think she did." "Not even casually?" "Nno . . ." and then she asked anxiously "Oh God, has something happened to Mr Twomey?" He struck a match, but his pipe was empty, yet he let the little flame wander towards his fingernail. "Why do you ask?" he watched her. She was much shaken. "I don't know," she said. "Did you expect that something might happen to Mr Twomey?" She stared at him. "No, why should I?" He took the box of matches out of his pocket again, and so I thought it was time to stop it, and I barked "Wwow!"'

'Good, it was high time to do so,' said the White Poodle.

'Thank you,' said the Black Poodle.

'That's all right,' said the White Poodle. 'Go on.'

'Well,' said the Black Poodle, 'so I barked "Wwow!" and she jumped up and exclaimed "Did you hear that? It must be Aaron!" and she ran upstairs, to Aaron's room, but he was peacefully asleep tucked up in his bed. I don't know what dreams he had because I didn't watch them, and then she went to the bedroom, opened the wardrobe, sniffed, and then looked down and saw me sitting there on the three pairs of shoes. That gave her another endocrine shock – so necessary for my purpose of transplanting her into a bigger flower-pot. "Good Lord!" she exclaimed . . .'

'Did she really?' asked the White Poodle.

'She did,' the Black Poodle answered. 'Such expressions as "piss off" she used only when she was with other people, when she was alone she would always say "Good Lord". And so she said "Good Lord" and then we went down and she said sternly "Mr Brown, I didn't know you had brought a dog with you. I found it in my wardrobe." And he said it wasn't his dog and could he inspect the wardrobe and she said "certainly not" and he bent down to look at me and saw a telephone number on my collar, so he went to the telephone, and she said "Will you please phone the station and ask them to bring Jolyon!" but he dialled the number that was on my collar and asked Have they lost a jet-black poodle-dog? and they said O yes, thank you, thank you very much, and could they come at once and fetch it, they live just round the corner, and in no time at all the bell rang and a male came in, six foot, eleven stone, black suit, white hair, and said "My name is Leech. How exceedingly kind, how very good of you to have taken all the trouble, Mrs Sheridan," and he moved towards me, and they expected me to jump up at him to greet him, but I took a step backwards and Mr Brown asked "Are you sure it is your poodle-dog?" and Mr Leech said "Of course I am, but he is a neuropath, and jealous, my wife is convinced that he understands every word one says, my wife and I had a little innocent exchange of views this morning which must have looked like a quarrel to him and upset him so much that he escaped and we couldn't find him." "What did you quarrel about?" asked Mr Brown. "I beg your pardon, Mr Sheridan?" said Mr Leech. "This is not Mr Sheridan, Mr Leech," she said, "this is Detective Constable Brown." "Detective *Sergeant*," he corrected her. "Oh . . ." said Mr Leech. "My sister has been arrested, and Sergeant Brown is making quite a fuss about it. All she did was go round in a motor-car with some silly transfers on the bonnet and proclaim a revolution." "Revolution?" asked Mr Leech. "For the freedom of printing four-letter words, for the sacred right to bring the four-letter word back to the masses!" "Oh . . ." said Mr Leech. "I would still like to know how your poodle found itself in the wardrobe in Mrs Sheridan's bedroom?" asked Mr Brown. "I say. . ." said Mr Leech. "And I should still like to know what your quarrel with your wife was about?" "Our exchange of views was on some abstract subjects, if you must know, Sergeant," said Mr Leech. "Oh," she exclaimed, "are you *Professor* Leech?" "Yes, I am. And I am very flattered to be known to you." "Oh, of course I know of you," she said. "When I was very young I read philosophy." "My dear lady . . ." he said, meaning that she was now very young. "I wish I hadn't," she said. "Oh?" Professor Leech said. "Well, what *is* philosophy?" she asked. "Philosophy isn't . . ." he started but she interrupted him: "I know what philosophy is not. But what is it? What does it reveal? My mother used to say, Everything is important, my girl. I have modified that slightly. I treat everything as though it may be important until such time as I find out whether it is or not. In my dream last night my mother would not have accepted this modification. Would you?" "Well, it all depends . . ." said Professor Leech. "I know it does," she said. "Actually, I must confess that the only thing I still remember of my studies is that last sentence, you know, the sacred Number 7. At my time it was the craze at all undergraduate parties.'"

'What was that Number 7?' the White Poodle asked.

'*Whereof one cannot speak, thereof one must be silent,*' said the Black Poodle.

'Oh,' said the White Poodle.

"'What is that Number 7?" asked the detective. But they were completely ignoring him by now. "Well," she said, "when I am teaching, I teach them some separate bits, and they do learn them, but I always fear that one day there will be a bright boy who will ask, What is it all about? And what will I do then? I feel as if I know thousands of separate pieces of a jigsaw-puzzle, I even know how to put some of them together, nevertheless, whenever I take a piece it falls down into a bottomless pit because I have nothing to put it *on*. Does your philosophy provide a table on which the jigsaw-puzzle could be laid out?" "Well, my dear lady, philosophy is not a religion," Professor Leech said. She now had her back turned to the detective and was speaking quickly, not to let him butt in. "And all this is because we are warm-blooded animals," she said. "When we were plants or fish we lived in unison with the environment, which was *around* us, the same for everybody; we had its temperature, its humidity, its everything. As soon as we became warm blooded, all this turned *inside out*, and now, what can be called 'environment' is in every one of us. It is *in* us that flow the rivers of blood, gales of oxygen, and erupt the volcanoes of endocrine secretion. The outside is cut off, by our clothes, walls, roofs, pavements, codes of behaviour. All that remained of Nature is within our skin. And when we crave to touch her with the other side of it, the only bits of her that we can still find are ourselves. So we undress and touch each other, anybody. Anybody," she repeated, and I thought it was time to act, so I barked, "Wwow Wwow" again and there was terrific lightning, a glorious roar of thunder and, in a second, the rain fell in floods upon the streets. And then the telephone rang. The detective moved towards it but Mrs Sheridan was ahead of him. "Yes?" she said. It was Mrs Leech. Could she speak to the professor? There was a twinkle in Mrs Sheridan's eye as, looking at Professor Leech, she said, "He has just left with the poodle." "Oh," said Mrs Leech, "it is raining so heavily, would Mrs Sheridan be so kind as to lend the professor an umbrella, he catches cold so easily!" "Yes, of course," said Mrs Sheridan, and then she went to the hall to fetch an umbrella, and Professor Leech went to the hall, and I produced another poodle who jumped and danced and begged to go with him, and Mrs Sheridan said to the detective "And now please go and send Jolyon here," and the detective said "I shall see what I can do, Mrs Sheridan," and they were all in the hall now, and they opened the door, and as they were going out into the downfall the two girls burst in, soaked through and happy, and they cried "Oh, don't shout at us, mummy," and she said "Of course not," and when the door was shut behind the detective and the professor, Charlotte said "Who are they, mummy? Are they your lovers?" and Harriet said "Which one?" and Charlotte said "Both?" and Harriet said "Do you have a lover?" and Mrs Sheridan said "I am not going to tell you," and Harriet said "Why not?" and Mrs Sheridan said "Because if I have a lover I don't want you to know that I have, and if I haven't I don't want you to know that I haven't," and Charlotte said "pity," and Mrs Sheridan said "Why?" and Charlotte said "Because I have a lover, and if you don't have one then you cannot understand how beautiful it is!" and all the time they were taking off their wet things, and Mrs Sheridan rubbed them with a towel, and then the girls ran to the kitchen and started cooking, and I kept the rain falling all the time, because I knew what I was doing, and I was right, because after a while Mrs Sheridan opened the front door, left it unlatched, and stepped out into the rain, and she stood there on the pavement and let herself get soaked through, and I warmed the rain a bit and narrowed it so that it didn't rain on her left and on her right but only where she was, and I purified it and made it *be* Nature, and she stood there, pretending to look and see whether her husband was coming back, but she was feeling it and taking it in with every pore of her skin, and what she thought was "Why do I think about him as *he* when I think about him, and don't think about him as *Tony*?" And then she thought "I don't know that if he knew as little about flying an aeroplane as he knows about political philosophy, and if he were at the controls, I would not go with him across the Channel. I know that if he knew as little about . . . ," then she said "But why should I not go with Tony in an aeroplane? What has the fact that the plane will crash to do with it?" and so I knew that I had already transplanted her to a bigger flower-pot, and I stopped the rain, and left her there in the street in front of the open door of her home, and I'm telling you, Don't touch her, leave her alone, because, whatever you say, and whatever He says, I shall not weed her out. Do you hear me, Poodle?!'

And the White Poodle answered: 'I am not a Poodle, I am a Lamb.' And he was.

THE FINISHING SCHOOL
OR
WHO FROM WHOM?

"Novelists often succeed where logicians fail," I said. She looked down on me.

"What do you know about logicians?" she sneered, in that polite, post-graduate, full of the pure-gold-of-intellectual-honesty, melodiously-arrogant voice.

Without getting up from my armchair, I took her by the elbows, turned her round, bent her over my knees. Lifted her skirt up, pulled her knickers down, and with the palm of my right hand measured three firm spanks on her buttocks. After which I pulled the knickers up and the skirt down. She lingered for a few seconds. But then she stood up and, facing me, said:

"You have committed two fallacies."

"Yes?"

"Firstly: you used force when you should have used arguments. Secondly: you meant it to be punishment, and it was pleasure."

*

It all started when Lady Cordelia Crab-Walker, parliamentary secretary to the Minister of Education, phoned me one morning and said: "Stefan darling, I need your help, – O, yes, it's immensely important – as soon as you can, there's a good boy – no, no, *not* in my office, the thing is top secret – of course, you silly – no, not that sort of 'top secret' – do you know that little place in Soho called 'Les Enfants Terribles'? it's either Dean Street or Wardour Street, never remember which – of course you do – will you invite me there for a cup of coffee at six o'clock? – that will be lovely – you *are* a poppet – what? – no, I didn't say 'a poppet', of course not, it must have been somebody on the line."

We were both five minutes late and, arriving from two opposite directions, met at exactly the same moment at the entrance to 'Les Enfants Terribles'. There were no more than three or four little tables in the café, but there was also a staircase leading down to the basement from which some psychedelic music was percolating upwards towards us. We stood at the top of the staircase, when the man behind the little coffee counter shook his head disapprovingly.

"No?" I asked.

"No," he said.

"He doesn't want us to go down to the basement," I explained to Cordelia.

"Why?" she asked.

"Apartheid," I said.

"What!" she exclaimed.

"Well," I said. "Age apartheid. The generation gap. He's terrified we might meet our own children there. Or grandchildren."

"So what if we do? I would like to. After all, I am the Ministry of Education. Good Lord!"

All the same, we didn't dive into the cellar, we sat politely in the corner by the window and ordered one *cappuccino* and one *espresso*.

"Well . . ." she looked straight into my eyes. *Her* eyes were wide open. They were green. With sparks of gold.

"Well," she said, "I want you to start something . . ." Keeping her eyes on me, she took the cup in her right hand, the saucer in her left, and took a sip of *cappuccino*. "I want you to start something from scratch. On a very low budget."

"To start what?" I asked.

She opened her mouth, and closed it, put down the saucer, and the cup, then folded her arms, and said firmly:

"A finishing school. Oh, don't blush! Not *that* sort of finishing school!" She shrugged her shoulders. "What we have decided is to open a finishing school for academic post-graduates. You see, the trouble with them is that they believe in what they have been taught, they believe that Truth is about statements, which it is, but they forget that statements are about the world, and it is truly extraordinary to observe how most of them, and especially the brilliant ones, and those from the best colleges, find themselves surrounded by a sort of unbridged moat as soon as they leave the groves of Academe and enter the bewildering world of life."

Her words seemed to me bewildering enough.

"And you want *me* to do the bridging?" I exclaimed. "How ridiculous, my dear Cordelia, and how naïve! Just imagine *me* taking them down the coal mines, or round the factory floors, or to Butlin's holiday camps!"

"Oh, no," she said calmly. "Those methods have already been tried, in other countries, without much success. What I want you to do is something different. I want you to take them back to what my dear friend Thomas Kuhn calls 'exemplars and paradigms'; I want you to make them – as my dear friend Steven Weinberg says – 'think abstractly and yet at the same time say something of relevance to concrete reality'; I want you – to give them back the ladder which they had rejected after having climbed up to the top shelf of abstraction, so that they could climb down to reality, in order to go up again strengthened by the experience."

"And how do you think I could do all that?" I asked.

"That" she said "we do not know. If we knew, we wouldn't have come to you, we would have gone to an expert."

*

That was how it happened that I found myself in the study of that government sponsored finishing school, spanking the sexy post-graduate lady's pink buttocks, which seemed to me prettier than her brain.

"You were wrong when you said that I should have used arguments," I said. "Arguments are for that part of the brain that is enclosed in your skull. But the brain doesn't end there. It runs down, all the way, down to your toes. And when what's going on in your skull starts turning round, faultlessly, back to the premises, and then, according to the rules of inference, forward to the same conclusion, like a gramophone needle stuck forever in the same groove, the best way to unstuck the brain is to hit that part of it which is in the bottom."

"Indeed," she said. "And what about that part of your brain that extends to the palm of your hand, which was in touch with my bottom, does it not affect the part that is in your skull?"

"Indeed it does," I said. "It affected it very pleasantly." And, before she had time to answer, I turned to the door, and shouted: "Next, please!"

Before the door opened, she still managed to scribble her telephone number on a piece of paper and to leave it on my desk.

*

The first thing I noticed when he opened the door was his dog-collar. Now, clergymen's dog-collars induce in me a picture of green fields, blue sky, flowers, a brook perhaps, a few chords of the Pastoral Symphony, little (not big) chirping birds, a quiet graveyard, peace, and good manners. That's why I was quite unprepared and taken by surprise when he marched furiously towards my desk, put both hands on its edge, bent over, and said with passion:

"I want you to attack me. I want you to tear me to pieces!"

Instinctively, my head moved a nose-length backwards.

"Won't you sit down," I proposed.

He didn't.

So I stood up.

It was simply ridiculous: two men facing each other across a desk and refusing to sit down. So I asked him my standard test-question: "Could you tell me what you would answer if somebody asked you what an electron is?"

"Free or bound?" he asked.

And he sat down.

And so did I.

He looked so young that if I had had some lollipops in my desk drawer, I would have been inclined to offer him one.

"I believe," he said. Full stop.

I nodded.

"I believe in God," he explained.

I nodded.

"Well," he said. "Come on, attack me, savage me, tear me to pieces."

"Why should I?" I asked.

"Why should you?" he repeated. "Do you not think that to believe is all wrong? Are you not . . ."

I stopped him.

"You have not come to discuss me," I said.

"No," he agreed. "I have not come here to discuss you. I have come here to discuss God."

"Oh Lord," I sighed.

"No need to jeer," he said. "So long as I lived *inter silvas academi,* I was in peace with him. I studied theoretical theology and I was not troubled by any inconsistencies that have been discussed by ecclesiastical philosophers. Well, you see, I studied theology and I studied physics. There is no discrepancy there. Physics is o.k. It is clean. You may even say beautiful. It is morally aseptic. Not so biology . . . But I didn't know that till I left the University."

"Did you study it afterwards?"

"I didn't study it. I *was* it. And either you understand what I mean or you don't. I can't explain it any further."

"Try," I said.

"Hell," he said. "The other day I saw on TV an Algerian who said he wanted to be a doctor but became a civil engineer. He couldn't force himself to study medicine, because – he said – when he was a schoolboy, there was a war in Algeria and he saw too much blood. It was the other way with me. I did my studies first, and saw too much blood later."

"Where?" I asked.

"How do you mean: where? Everywhere. Every-bloody-where! As soon as I left the cozy Shangri-la of the Alma Mater, I saw that the whole God-made world is built on the Principle of Devouring; each cubic inch of the God-made soil – a battlefield or a slaughterhouse."

"Are you a vegetarian?" I asked.

"No," he said. "I'm not. One cannot be against suffering death if, without it, there cannot be life. But I do say to myself, as all Christians must have done, at one time of their life or another: If it was God's aim to make His little creatures suffer, then He is not good. On the other hand, if their suffering is what He uses for some of His higher aims, it follows that He can't achieve those aims by any other means and, if so, there must be some laws which He must obey and, if so, they, the Laws, are greater than He is and, again, if so, it is they, the Laws, that are God."

He was out of breath.

"Is it in Him that you are losing your faith, or in His attributes?" I asked.

"Neither," he burst out. "And that's what puzzles me. Why don't I? That's incomprehensible. Why do I want to cling to it? Why do I want to be sure that it is as strong as ever? Because that's why I want to put it to the test. That's why I'm asking you to attack me, savage me, tear me to pieces. I want to stand up to all your atheistic blows."

"Don't be silly," I said. "I haven't the slightest intention of fighting it out with you."

"But . . ." he started. "But they told me . . ."

"Go to hell," I said. "And don't tell me what they told you. Whoever they are. You assume that I don't believe because I'm not puzzled. The truth is just the opposite, I'm puzzled too much to believe in anything. The old man with a white beard sitting on a cloud, or the Big Bang."

"Puzzled by what?" he asked.

"Puzzled by everything. By you and by a grain of sand, by the galaxies and by a butterfly. Puzzled by the fact that there is something rather than nothing. By the fact that the world is not a perfect sphere of emptiness, a perfect symmetry of nothingness. You see I'm *more* puzzled than you are, and that's precisely why I cannot accept any of your beliefs."

"They've sent me to the wrong chap," he said.

"They have," I agreed. "They've sent me the wrong chap. When they send me the right kind of chaps, I tell me: 'Now, as you have left the University and entered the real Universe, you must stop fidgeting and start thinking!' For you, however, I have a different message: 'Stop thinking about Great Becauses and Great Aims and try, simply, to be nice."

"How do you mean – nice?"

"Nice. Decent. Forget your theology, and practise the art of being nice. To your parishioners. To other people, And to yourself."

"You sound like one of those flower-children," he said.

"That's the greatest compliment anybody has ever paid me," I said.

"You devil," he said, and got up.

I got up.

We were facing each other across the desk. He stretched out his hand to grasp mine. I didn't notice that he was left-handed. His left hand and my right didn't fit.

"Next, please," I shouted, as he opened the door and left.

*

The next arrival was a young bearded man, a graduate. "Won't you sit down?" I said. He did. And started fiddling with his long hair.

Perhaps because I was still tired and couldn't invent anything new, or perhaps because I thought it was, in fact, quite successful, I asked my standard test question:

"Could you tell me what you would answer if somebody asked you what an electron is?"

"Electron?" he repeated and looked around anxiously. "Electron? *You* can't possibly mean those little things they tell you about in physics? Electron? It must be masculine of Electra. She loved her father and hated her mother. Therefore Electron must have loved his mother and hated his father. Therefore Electron must be a synonym of Oedipus."

He was a nice young man, and I found his knowledge of mythology and psychology quite impressive, but he wouldn't tell me what it was that had made him join the Finishing School. "Well," I recapitulated after an hour and a quarter, "all right. Once upon a time you had an affair with a boy. And you had an affair with a dog, And you had an affair with yourself. That's fine. But did you ever have an affair with a woman?"

He shook his head.

So I took the scrap of paper on which the beautiful blonde post-graduate had written her telephone number, and I gave it to him.

*

The moment he came in, I knew there was some mistake. Firstly, because he was so old. Not as old as I am, not many people nowadays are, nevertheless nobody of his age could possibly wish to be a finishing school pupil. And secondly, because I knew who he was. Yes, somebody must have directed him to the wrong door.

He noticed my unease and interpreted it correctly.

"I hope," he said, when we had exchanged some preliminary courtesies, "I hope the fact that I graduated some 25 years ago will not disqualify me for your finishing school and thus rob me of the benefits of your tutorship."

"I don't see why it should," I said. "But wouldn't it be rather absurd? You, with your great experience and knowledge of the world . . ."

"It is kind of you to take that line," he interrupted me, "but you know very well that I wouldn't have come here were I not sure that I would profit by doing so. And what you have just said confirms that I was not mistaken: you said 'experience and knowledge of the world'. By using these two words instead of one you have already put me on the right track. Well, my dear sir, as you must know, I make occasional speeches in the Upper House, they are recorded in Hansard, and sometimes I manipulate words so that they make people sit up and take notice. I am also active in the City. There I manipulate money by pushing it from one place to another and back again, and, you could say, rolling in it, though I don't even see it. Now, all this may look very impressive from the outside, but I, in my inner guts, I know that there is something hollow, a vesicle of void, an air-pocket, a vacuum, both in my words and in money. "Oh, no," with a gesture he shut me up before I had time to open my mouth, "I know what you are going to say, my dear sir," he announced. "You are going to say that both words and money are symbols, and that I am manipulating them according to the Coherence Theory of Truth, so that they would be consistent with each other like pieces of a jigsaw puzzle, and that I don't give a damn for the Correspondence Theory of Truth which would insist that my speech acts and my finance acts should portray or represent some facts. Well, you see, I know all that, and I'm not asking you for a diagnosis, I'm asking for a cure. And I trust you will prescribe something less naïve than paying a visit to a widowed shareholder in her drawing room, or to some hard-working fisherman in a seaside resort."

"All right," I said. "But first I want to ask you a question."

"By all means, go ahead, do," he said.

"Well," I said, "tell me what you would answer if somebody asked you what an electron is."

He was taken aback, though he tried not to show it.

"Let me see," he said. "Electron? That's an adoption of the Greek word ηλεχτρον meaning *amber,* isn't it?"

I laughed.

"There you are," I said. "How typical! You look for the meaning of a word in its past. As if The Good Lord, at the time of His Almighty Big Bang, also created the Omniscient Oxford English Dictionary, a verbal pool of concepts valid for ever and ever Amen."

His upper lip kept stiff under the grey mustachio.

"All right," I said, "my advice is to lay the Amber Dictionary aside, and . . ."

"And what?" he asked scornfully, "and take to electronics?"

"No," I said. "And be an eagle."

He spread his arms, looked at me sharply from under his bushy eyebrows and, reassured, said:

"Oh, I see what you mean! To soar! Up to the vaulted roof! Like prices on the market!"

"You express it better than I could," I said.

"Naturally," he said. "Of course, I am a professional speaker. And I am good at it. And a good professional speaker knows what's in the mind of his listeners. It is his business to know and to express it for them. Especially if they are good listeners. And you are a marvellous listener. I know what you were just going to say. You were going to say that I am a liberal progressive. Tory, endowed with a social conscience. That I like to use such words as *tolerance, democracy, progress, evolution, ideology, christianity, alienation.* That I manipulate these words with Rhetorical Coherence in the Upper House, just as I manipulate figures with Arithmetical Coherence in the City. But – you were going to ask me – What if the World is *not* coherent? Anyway, not in my linguistic way? What then? What do I do when they find themselves in such a world? And what do I do with then? I shut my eagle eyes and say *Tolerance.* But do I ask myself the question: Can the view-that-all-views-must-be-tolerated contain the view that the-view-that-all-views-must-be-tolerated cannot be tolerated? I say *Democracy.* But when I say Democracy, do I not mean: majority rule? And is that not tyranny? Exercised by the sacred cow of the majority? Shouldn't I rather advocate the Tolerance of minorities? Because *Progress* is evolutionary, and *Evolution* rises to the stepping-stones of mutants, and mutants are always in the minority. Now, I praise *Ideologies.* But do they not cause hatred and violence? Is not the common Decency of Means the essence of all utopian dreams? And thus, is not the Decency of Means the Aim of Aims? And so you are right, My Rhetorical Coherence, which you can find in Hansard, is *not* the same Coherence that is (if at all) in the World. And so, to her I glorify *Christianity.* Yet, isn't Marxism a wish to translate Christianity into the language of practical deeds?" He stopped, overwhelmed by his own brilliance. And then paraphrased:

"Is not Marxism the continuation of Christianity by other means?"

"Bravo!" I said.

"Or take *Alienation*. It is so that some people are alienated from the Establishment, or is the Establishment that alienates itself from people?"

"Bravo!" I repeated.

"You shouldn't clap your hands," he corrected me. "These are *your* thoughts not mine. I am only formulating them for you, as I said I would." He paused, wagged his finger at me, and added warningly: "But *you* mustn't go about putting such thoughts into people's heads."

"Why not?" I asked.

"Well," he said. "Don't be childish. You know perfectly well that people talk about your school. They say Cordelia was mad to start a thing like that. They say it's irresponsible. They say it allows too much freedom of speech."

"And you agree . . ."

"Look here, we are all for freedom of speech, but not necessarily at the expense of the tax-payer."

"But we are all tax-payers," I protested, "and rate payers and VAT payers."

He laughed.

"Oh, don't be ridiculous. How much do you pay? Peanuts in comparison with the fortune I give each year to the tax-gatherers."

"So you think that we should have our freedom of speech in proportion to the income-tax we pay?"

He jumped up.

"That's an idea! Don't claim copyright on it because I'm going to use it."

CODA
(or It's for me to decide who's alienated from whom, I from you, or you
from me)

"Meet another philosopher," said Edith at Bertie's birthday party. So they agglamourated aground me, bright twitching integrogation marks in their eyes: "Where from? Where from? From where?," *meaning:* the womb of which Alma Mater feeds you with her milch juice for teaching young beasts what you have learned from old lizards, *meaning:* whom have you unsaddled, O unknown reptile; for the vacating of whose chair are you lying in wait, *meaning:* are we going to beg you to notice us, or is it you who is going to beg us to notice you; come on, quick, quick tell us, quick, quick, because neither social intercourse nor academic evolutionary processes are possible without that bit of information: quick, "where from? where from? from where?""From Erehwon," I said. Their bristles, their quills, their fishscales hedgehogged. Tiny, miniature, electronically lit geographical globuses were turning round quickly in their searching eyeballs. Erewhat?, where was it? They tried to remember what geography they had learnt ten, twenty, thirty years ago at school. "From *where*?" they repeated. "From Nowhere." I explained; and thought: if I deserved to carry the name of philosopher, which place to have come from would be more appropriate than a place which is independent of any longitude, or latitude, or altitude, creditude, but I had no time to develop the thought because at this moment one of the blackjacketed teachers shoved forward his arm, – and the well-groomed stiff index finger, and the ring on it, and the hand, and the wrist, went through my chest, effortlessly, as if I were composed of the air that surrounded me. Which is as it must be, because if you come from nowhere then it is logically necessary that wherever you are you are nowhere, because if there were anywhere a borderline such that jumping over it could transfer you to this side of it, then nowhere would have to be on the other side of the borderline and, being there, it would be somewhere, which is not compatible with being nowhere, and thus, consequently, once you are nowhere, nowhere you are wherever you are, the only meaning of which is that you are indistinguishable from what is around you, pierceable by what is around is pierceable by; if it is air, if you are submerged in water then you are water, if you are buried up to your armpits while your head is in the centre of a soundwave, then you are earth up to your armpits and a scream from your armpits up. The blackjacketed teachers made unequal numbers of steps backwards, three steps, one step, two steps, and the zaubercircle was no more a circle, it broke behind me and its loose ends globetrotted away to akimbo around another point on the parquet floor. Well, they had to be somewhere. They would feel lost anywhere else. It is only I who nowhere am lost and feel at home everywhere. I feel at home in any child's cot, in any woman's bed, in any corpse's coffin. I feel at home with viruses in the guts of a louse, and with lice in a dove's feathers, and with doves in the heart of Jesus. Goodnight chums. Goodnight everybody. Goodnight.

PLAY

THE BONE IN THE THROAT

SCENE ONE

Before the curtain rises, – a single note on the piano. A large hall in a country house. The house must be standing on the slope of a hill, as you can see treetops through the window on the left, but the garden through the window on the right. In the middle of the wall, between the windows, a portrait of a judge. It is probably a portrait of Cecil ffahrenheit himself. There are seven chairs beneath the portrait.

On the left, an opening – perhaps between two columns or under an arch – leading to further rooms. Nearer the footlights, a door. On the right, half the height of the stage, a gallery, or shall we call it a balcony. There are two doors there: to Steve's room, upstage, and to Mary's room, downstage. The staircase to the gallery runs along the wall. It consists of two flights, the upper flight facing the audience, the lower flight facing away from the audience. There is a piano beneath the lower flight. John is sitting at it, his back to the audience. He is about 18. The entrance door is on the right, half hidden by the staircase. An immense chandelier hangs right in the centre of the hall.

Diana comes in through the door on the right. She is a few years over, but looks just under forty. She is in riding breeches, jacket, and long, muddy boots, and she carries a double-barrelled gun. Her costume suits her. As she enters, she steps on two square pieces of felt that have been placed by the door for the purpose, and skates on them across the parquet floor.

DIANA

Glorious Day!

She moves across the room on the felt.

John strikes one, single note, listens to it attentively, after a while, strikes another.

DIANA

The wind and the sun.

Puts the gun in the corner by the left window, and skates back.

DIANA

The sun bakes you while the wind blows the heat off your skin. Like those gadgets at the hairdresser's, you know.

She sits in the armchair, rings the bell.

John strikes a Webernian chord.

Nelson enters, kneels in front of Diana, ready to help her take her boots off.

DIANA
(Stands up)

John! Listen to me, John. You know if your Father could see you there, sitting in that dark corner doing nothing, he would turn in his grave three times. That's to say, if he were dead and buried.

JOHN

Will you please leave Father alone.

DIANA

(Mockingly)

Will you please leave Father alone!
(She sits down again and gives her boot to Nelson)

DIANA

As if it were not *he* who left me alone!
(Sarcastically)
Alone! With you, and Mary, and Steve!

JOHN

Mary? Who's Mary?

DIANA

What did you say?

JOHN

I said: Who is Mary? Is she somebody one should know? And . . . incidentally, who is Steve? Is he somebody worth talking about?

DIANA

(Kicks her boot across the room, it hits the piano)

John!

NELSON

(Going to fetch the boot)

Cook said that the bird was shot right through the heart. It must have fallen like a stone. She asks whether she shall prepare it for tomorrow's dinner.

DIANA

No. I don't want to see it. Tell her to keep it for the kitchen.

(To John)

"Who is Steve? Who is Mary?"! Indeed!

(Calling)

Steve! Mary!

(Nelson pulls off her other boot and gives her her slippers)

Steve! Mary!

The doors on the balcony open – Steve appears in one, Mary and the Rev. Fred Oosky in the other. Mary is 19, Steve 17. The Rev. Fred Oosky belongs to their generation rather than to Diana's, but his status makes him her contemporary, almost.

STEVE

Is the house on fire?

MARY

Shut up, Steve.

(To Diana)

Did you have a nice time?

DIANA

It doesn't matter now.

(To Nelson)

That will be all, Nelson, thank you.

Exit Nelson. Mary comes down the stairs, Mr. Oosky follows her. Steve sits on the balcony, his legs dangling in the air.

DIANA

I wanted to talk to you about John. He has invented a new method to drive *me* mad.

JOHN

Now we're going to start all over again. Hell! Can't one ever have any peace here?

(To Diana)

You like an open air aloneness. I like to be alone within four walls. You have already had your peace in the woods this morning, shooting the bird right through the heart. You always shoot them right through the heart. Why can't I have my peace here, under the stairs?

DIANA

Be reasonable, John, I didn't disturb your peace. I came in, bright and happy, and said: What a glorious day. Whereupon you asked: Who is Mary, and who is Steve? It's idiotic!

STEVE

Why did you ask who I am?

JOHN

I didn't ask it like that . . . She . . .

DIANA

John!

JOHN

Mother . . .

DIANA
(Stamping her foot)

John!

JOHN

All right – *Diana* . . . said something about Steve and Mary, and you aren't the only Steve and Mary in the world, are you? So I asked . . .

STEVE
(To Diana)

What did you say about us?

DIANA

Nothing. I don't remember.

MARY

Then try to remember.

DIANA

Oh, leave me alone.

JOHN

She said she was left alone with me and you, so, naturally I asked her who you were.

STEVE

You're crazy!

JOHN

I don't see why. Absolutely anybody can be Steve or Mary. How could I know she . . .

DIANA

John!

JOHN

How could I know you were not talking about your horses. Come on, Steve! Come on, Mary! Or about your hounds? Or about your lovers?

Mary drops down on to her knees as if she wanted to say a prayer.

Mr. Oosky impatiently pulls her up.

DIANA

(Silvery, uninhibited laughter)

Hahaha! You all seem to be deeply shocked, "lovers," hahaha! You know, my dears, at moments like this I always feel as if I were standing in front of my grandparents, and not my own children. I'm not talking about you, Mr. Oosky, but these sensitive, dried-up flowers, . . . if Father could see you now, he would turn . . .

JOHN

I asked you to leave Father alone.

DIANA

All right, all right, my pet. I suppose it's modern education that makes you all so priggish. I suppose that three immature, weakly creatures must be considered more important than a grown-up, healthy woman.

(She seems to grow taller)

I have been left alone with my lovers.

(She takes off her riding jacket)

My body, the same body which produced you, the three of you, is not a factory. It is not a chemical factory. A part of the I.C.I. combine.

(She puts on the red gown that has been brought by Nelson with her slippers)

My body is an animal. And I like animals. I look after animals. I will allow no one to deprive them of the sustenance they need.

(She takes off her riding breeches, under her gown, and puts them beside the jacket on the armchair)

I give it what it needs, and I don't let it pine away and adulterate the clarity of my vision. And if you don't like it, you can go psychoanalyse yourselves.

(To Mr. Oosky)

Do you approve?

OOSKY

I approve of half of what you say. But I admire it in its entirety.

(He moves towards her. He is now in the centre of the room. Right under the chandelier.)

You are great, Diana. However, you don't realise, perhaps, how difficult it is for your children to live in a world dominated by your personality . . .

DIANA

I am as much a part of the world they find around them as they are a part of the world I find around me. But . . . But perhaps I'm blind. Perhaps I don't see what I'm doing. If that is so, please tell me. Am I a bad mother?

STEVE

No, Mummy . . .

DIANA

Steve!

STEVE

No, Diana, You are wonderful. But you are so old-fashioned.

DIANA

Old-fashioned? I?

MARY

You don't believe in God.

DIANA
(Reluctantly)

Yes . . . ?

(Turns to Steve)

STEVE

You say Russian Sputniks are progress.

DIANA
(Turning to John)

You have already made your accusation.

John shuts the piano with a bang. Steve puts his legs through the banister rails and starts swinging them. Mary, facing Mr. Oosky, silently tries out some twisting.

DIANA

Well, if you say so, I am old-fashioned. I got up at dawn, when you were still ruminating the ancient vapours of your modern dreams,

I cooked myself a nice, smelly breakfast of eggs and bacon, (it was too early to wake Mrs. Shepherd up) and, yes, you may think it shocking to do such a thing at that hour, but I poured myself a glass of old-fashioned whiskey instead of sucking your coca cola through a double-barrelled plastic straw. By that time I had finished with my copy of The Times, and with the Daily Mirror as well. You may not know that the Daily Mirror is delivered to our house every morning, for Cook; her husband is a candidate for the rural council, I don't know if you are aware of it, a very left-wing candidate, and I am going to vote for him. Not that his sympathies are mine, but I feel loyal to Cook, if you see what I mean. No, you don't. Anyway, at the time when your modern sub-consciousness was turning your earthly desires into silly symbols, I was writing instructions to Miss Penfold to renew my subscription to the New Statesman; to send a cheque to Father Huddleston; and to write to Earl Russell asking him to add my signature to his open letter against the H-Bomb. After which I took my horse and rode across the fields to The Brambles; the sun by then was just on top of . . . – however, a description of the scenery would bore you (beyond measure), it's enough to say that, when on the other side of the lake, I had a . . . Revelation. Suddenly, without any premonition, I *saw* what to answer my stockbroker who has been pestering me for a decision about my Anglo-Iranian shares. After that I recited to myself, from memory, a poem I had read in the Evergreen Review, a poem by a plaintive San Francisco beatnik-monk, then I shot the bird, I shot it straight through the heart, it dropped like a . . .

MARY

Mummy, please . . .

DIANA

. . . a stone. I inhaled the morning air, I rode back home, took the bird to the kitchen, apologised to the staff for the mess you left after your last night's party, came here, said old-fashionedly: 'What a glorious day!', upon which you dragged me into an idle modern conversation which is nothing but neurotic nonsense.

MARY

If we are neurotics, it is your fault.

DIANA

Mine?

STEVE

She means: your generation's.

JOHN

You didn't prevent the war.

DIANA

Quite so. I'm sorry. I, Diana ffahrenheit, didn't prevent the war. It was very negligent of me, and I apologise . . . Incidentally, are you of the opinion that I should have tried to prevent the war by being *against* it or by being *for* it? Some people think that being *for* would have prevented the last war. What do you think? Nothing? Do you know that when war was approaching I was your present age? Why don't you do something to prevent the next one?

JOHN

It's different.

DIANA

Yes, I suppose it is. When I was a child, I thought I was what I would have become. So I looked towards the future to see what I was. And so every moment of my life became the dawn of a tomorrow. I expected things to happen, and still do. It's different with you. You seem to think that you are what you have become; so in order to find out who you are, you look backwards and treat the present moment of your lives as if they were sunsets of yesterday. At your age!

MARY

Mummy! If you say another word, I shall scream. Sunsets or not sunsets, you know that if something in a machine has got into a mess, the first thing you have to do is put it right.

DIANA

A mended machine is a second-hand machine.

JOHN

You hate us! You simply hate us!

DIANA

No, John. But one doesn't mend a biological machine. One lets it grow. And you are wrong if you think that I hate you. I don't. I love you. I love you as you are. And I want you to grow into the future from where you are now, as you are. Why don't you come into the open, John, and make love to a pretty country girl? No, you sit at your piano, strike solitary notes, and indulge in the pleasure of hearing the vibrations of a single string. Interesting, but somewhat disappointing.

(She turns to Mary)

And you Mary, your Christian faith is like John's music. It is thin. Why don't you ask Mr. Oosky to rape you? Your virginity . . .

OOSKY

You misunderstand both Mary's feelings and my intentions.

DIANA

Perhaps . . .

STEVE

You haven't yet preached to me, Diana. Not that I particularly . . .

DIANA

To you, Steve, but you simply don't exist. You don't exist except in your gang. There, yes, I admit. I saw you roaring on your motorbike. In your gang you're brave and quite somebody. Without your pals, however, you are nothing. Alone with the Universe, you don't know what to do with your hands and your legs. Why? Why can't you break something and take the consequences when you are without your pals? Well, I'm going to have a hot bath now.

Exit Diana, through the door on the left. Pause.

Mary, followed by Mr. Oosky, goes up the stairs to her room. Then Steve gets up and goes to his room. John alone. He gets up, crosses the room, stops at the armchair, picks up Diana's riding breeches with his left hand, her jacket with his right. Pause. Puts down the breeches. Lifts the jacket and smells it. As if he wants to check whether something he has read in his books is true or not. It seems not to have the expected effect on him. He puts it down. Walks to the window. Looks out. Sits down on one of the seven chairs at the back wall. Gets up and sits on another. Ditto and ditto. And again, slowly and methodically. He tries all the *chairs. Parlour maid, a puzzled expression on her face, enters through the door on the right. She had the puzzled expression <u>before</u> she noticed John. John goes up and tries to embrace her.*

MAID

Not now. I'm busy. Is your mother expecting anybody, do you know? There's a gentleman there who looks as if he has been invited to stay.

JOHN

Mother is in her bath. Go and ask her.

Clock strikes noon. Exit maid through door on left. John walks up and down. Stops under the chandelier. Walks back to the piano. Sits down. Opens the lid.

MAID

(Re-entering)

She doesn't remember, but says she can't be sure.

She crosses the stage. John catches her, smells her hair, she frees herself, climbs the stairs, knocks on the first door (Mary's), and then goes straight to the second door and knocks. Steve opens it, she asks him about the visitor, inaudibly; he evidently doesn't know anything about it. The first door opens, Mary in it – ditto. Both doors shut. Maid goes down, John is now at the piano, Maid crosses the stage and exists through the door on the left. John strikes one note on the piano and listens to its sound attentively for a long while. Maid comes back, crosses the stage quickly, disappears through the door on the right and at once appears again, letting in Mr. Barnum. He is Diana's age. It is not known whether he has ever served with the R.A.F., but he has that kind of moustache and manner. Maid feels awkward about the two suitcases he is carrying, but he doesn't let her touch them. He stands right under the chandelier.

SCENE TWO

MAID

Madam says would you excuse her, sir; she will be with you in a moment.

(Exit)

Mr. Barnum throws a short glance at the chandelier. After a while, lifts his head again and looks at it pensively, when suddenly John strikes another note.

BARNUM

(Startled)

How do you do, sir! I apologise, I didn't notice your presence. My name is Barnum, Joshua Hieronymous Barnum.

Diana has entered during this sentence. She is in tweeds now, but her hair is still as it was when she was in her bath.

DIANA

(Who has evidently heard the same, comes towards Mr. Barnum, her arm extending to shake hands)

I hope you had a nice journey, Mr. Barnum.

BARNUM

(Very rapidly)

I have indeed. Admirable! I love travelling by country buses. Though sometimes I miss one. As I did this morning. Which is the reason for my arriving half an hour later . . .

JOHN

Later than what?

BARNUM

Later than I would have done otherwise. How strange! N'est-ce pas? Whenever somebody misses a bus, I ask myself: How many subsequent events would have taken a different course if he had caught it? So much of the fate of so many people is the outcome of such simple things as misread bus timetables, n'est-ce pas? And I missed mine just by a split second. My foot was already on the step. But with these heavy things to carry . . .

DIANA

I must call Nelson to take care of your suitcases, Mr. Barnum. I am . . .

She turns towards the bell, but stops eagerly when Mr. Barnum protests.

BARNUM

Oh no no no no! It's quite all right. Besides, they are not suitcases. Not really. Though what I intend to say was something different. Suppose I lift my foot

(he demonstrates)

at a certain moment, and suppose it is the very last moment in which I can board the bus. Now, suppose I left my foot again, and suppose it is the very first moment in which I am bound to miss it.

Do you follow me?

MARY

DIANA

I follow you with pleasure.

BARNUM

Well, how big do you think is the split second between those two moments? It cannot be nothing, because then the two moments would be one and the same moment, which is not possible, because we cannot at the same time both board a bus and miss it. On the other hand, the distance between the two moments cannot be so big that we could divide it in two. Because if there were room for us to be in between, we should be both too late to board the bus and too early to miss it.

Mary, who a short while before entered through her door and is now coming down the stairs, followed by Mr. Oosky, as previously, misses her step and stumbles. At that moment Steve enters, looks round anxiously, then sits down on the floor of the balcony, his legs dangling in the air as before.

MARY
(To nobody)

Damn!

OOSKY
(To nobody)

High heels!

DIANA

Mr. Barnum, the young lady who has just fallen down the stairs and is reclining now on the floor is my daughter Mary. The shadow you see behind her is the Reverend Fred Oosky. The rubber soles dangling in the air belong to my son Steve. And you have already met, I think, my other son John and his musical box.

(They howdoyoudo each other)

Mr. Barnum was just telling us about his idea of time. Were you not, Mr. Barnum? He thinks Time is not a River, but a String of Pearls. Very minute pearls. But unbreakable.

OOSKY

How very interesting!

BARNUM

Thank you . . .

MARY

(To Diana)

Unbreakable! I might have broken my leg and you wouldn't even have noticed.

BARNUM

(To Diana)

You put it in a nutshell.

DIANA

(To Mary)

I would, darling.

BARNUM

(To Diana)

Take, for instance, Matter.

DIANA
(To Mary)
But you wouldn't have broken your leg. Nothing ever happens to you.

MARY
(To Mr. Barnum)
I am *not* interested in Matter.

BARNUM
Exactly. We divide Matter into atoms. But as soon as we try to divide atoms, they become something else: waves, energy, linguistic problems. Anything but Matter. So why be interested in it?

DIANA
(To Mary)
Sometimes I wish you *would* break your leg and grow up.

BARNUM
In my humble opinion, something very similar happens to Time. You can divide it into a String of Pearls.
(He bows to Diana)
But if you try to cut a single pearl in two, it ceases to be a pearl of Time and becomes something else.

DIANA

What?

BARNUM
I don't know. It's up to the scientists to find out.

MARY

Pooh!

STEVE
(To Mr. Barnum)

Are you a scientist?

DIANA
(Reproach)

Steve!

Steve stops dangling his legs and draws them back.

OOSKY

I have already said that your theory is interesting. Yet, before I subscribe to it, I need to know what is its bearing on Eternity and the Immortality of the soul.

Steve sticks his legs out and starts swinging them again.

BARNUM

I'm afraid I couldn't commit myself as far as that. But I *can* tell you why wolves howl at the full moon.

DIANA

How exciting! Won't you sit down, Mr. Barnum?
(She sits in her armchair)

BARNUM
(Sits on his two cases)

Thank you.

John strikes E flat on the piano.

BARNUM
(Listens attentively, then says)

E flat.

JOHN

Correct.
He strikes G.

BARNUM
(As before)

G.

John approves, and strikes F and F sharp simultaneously three times.

BARNUM

F and F sharp!

DIANA

John! Can't we have a single second without being disturbed by an excerpt from Webern? Mr. Barnum is going to tell us how his theory of Time and Mr. Oosky's Immortality of the soul combine to make wolves howl at the full moon. It must be extremely interesting.

BARNUM

Precisely. You've put my point in a nutshell, Mrs. ffahrenheit. N'est-ce pas?

STEVE

Are you French?

BARNUM

No, why?

MARY

Shut up, Steve,

STEVE

Are you a Jew?

DIANA

Steve, how can you? There has never been a single Jew in this house. I wouldn't know one if I saw one.

(To Mr. Barnum)

You mustn't pay any attention to my children, Mr. Barnum. They are so Aristotelian, or is it Platonic? Steve thinks that everything one talks about exists. Especially if it is talked about in the newspapers. Mary thinks that everything she can feel exists, especially if it comes from her glands. John thinks that everything he does exists, especially if it is something of short duration and which dissolves, like his music, in the air. They have read neither Earl Russell nor Count Korzybski, Mr. Barnum. All they read is Wittgenstein and Sartre. "Intimacy," you know. People say that there is more depth in Sartre, but I know all the gossip about Professor Ayer and I think he is more bottomless. Are you comfortable where you are, Mr. Barnum?

BARNUM

I am, thank you.

DIANA

Then pray continue.

BARNUM

(Draws out the end of an electric cord from a side compartment of his white suitcase and goes with it to an electric outlet in the wall)

Two hundred and forty?

STEVE

Yeah!

Mr. Barnum inserts the plug. The sound of an electric motor swells and then fades as Mr. Barnum pulls out the plug.

BARNUM

(Coiling up the wire and putting it back into the compartment of the suitcase)

This is, more or less, how the wolf howls.

(Pause)

The point is, you see, that dead bodies smell.

OOSKY

They do.

BARNUM

And neither men nor wolves like the smell of dead bodies.

OOSKY

A slight whiff of the smell men *may* like, especially if it is mixed with the smell of incense. But I don't know about wolves.

BARNUM

I know about wolves. I know everything about wolves. They just simply hate it. Look how they *eat*. They don't eat, they shut their eyes and they *devour*. To get rid of the bloody delicious flesh as fast as possible. And not to leave a trace to go bad. The very expectation of smelling the smell of dead bodies makes them sick. The anaerobic process of decomposing proteins . . .

MARY

Mr. Barnum, if you say another word I shall scream!

BARNUM

Precisely. That is precisely how *they* feel. You see, it is all right when they are really hungry. When they are really hungry, nothing will stop them from killing and eating. It is also all right when their stomachs are full; nothing prevents them then from going away from the smell they don't like. It is only somewhere in between, when they are hungry enough to want to eat but not hungry enough to ignore the expectation of the smell, that they are torn by their own nervous system into two opposite directions; the result is that their whole inside begins to tremble and vibrate, and this trembling and vibration focuses on their larynx, and when a gasp of air passes through it, it is given the shape of this vibration, and it is this shape, this column of trembling air, that we call the wolf's howling.

(Pause)

We could as well call it a hymn, a psalm, or a prayer.

OOSKY

(Reproachfully)

Mr. Barnum!

BARNUM

(Confidentially, or conspiratorially, to Mr. Oosky)

It's all right, Mr. Oosky.

He is standing now. He glances at his watch. He has made a long journey, and hasn't yet heard any indication that he'll be invited to lunch. He is evidently hungry. He swallows, sniffs the air, looks at the door. Then resumes his talk. He is an old actor playing Hamlet, but only for a fraction of a second.

BARNUM

For wolves, it is: to kill, or not to be.

(Pause)

Yet "to kill" means: decomposed proteins – and decomposed proteins mean the smell they hate. This particular smell to the wolf is like the word "death" to us. And the smell "death" for a wolf, like the word "death" for us, spells "not to be, or not to be," and the wolf feels baffled by this, his own, particular physiological linguistics; he feels trapped by this language of smells and actions; he neither knows a logical positivist who would tell him that the smell is *not* the thing it represents, nor has he a priest to teach him when it is moral to suppress one's nausea and kill, and when it is not. It is not too bad during the day time. In day time there are so many things going on in the wood to detract his attention from this conflict.

(With sudden depth of feeling)

But when the night has come, the wolf sits on his hind legs and doesn't understand; or, if you prefer it, feels that something is wrong, feels some lack of logic. If he has been created a carnivorous animal, as he has, why is he endowed with that dislike of the smell of decomposed proteins, the smell of death? And if he is created allergic to the smell, why can't he survive on grass, or minerals? He can't answer the question. Who could? He feels he is *the bone in the throat* of God, he feels he is the marrow of Universal Tragedy, the centre of Eternal Conflict, and when the full moon rises in the black sky and pulls his eyes toward her pale face, his throbbing larynx produces the howl which, for him, replaces what, for us, would be a doleful lay, or a philosophical treatise, or a theological dissertation.

MARY
(Who for some time now has been cruising around the suitcases, trying to find out what they are, stops and says sweetly)
Mr. Barnum, wouldn't you be more comfortable on one of those chairs?

BARNUM
(Get up, becoming himself again)
Oh? Thank you.

While he moves upstage, Mary lightly kicks the cases, and finds they are very heavy. She is now standing between them, and right below the chandelier.

MARY
(To herself)
Good heavens!

OOSKY
What is it?

MARY
I don't know. My intuition told me something, but I seem to have become too civilized to understand what it was.

DIANA
(To Mr. Barnum, rather sternly)
Mr. Barnum, I must ask you a question.

BARNUM

(To Diana)

Please do *not*. It isn't that I don't want to answer it. I will. But . . .

MARY

(To Mr. Barnum)

I don't believe w . . .

DIANA

But?

STEVE

(To Diana)

Ask him if he's a zoo keeper.

DIANA

But?

BARNUM

(Continuing)

You see, my wife . . .

DIANA

(To Mr. Barnum)

Your wife . . . ?

MARY

(Louder)

Mr. Barnum, I don't believe w . . .

BARNUM
(Continuing)

I'm sure my wife is . . .

DIANA

Oh, you should have been asked to come with your wife; I'm so sorry.

BARNUM

I'm sure my wife is now sitting in her room in Dolphin Square, dreaming of a mink coat, as usual, . . . and

DIANA
(Shocked)

A mink coat? No!

BARNUM

You see? And my child is playing with her hula-hoop, and they are waiting . . .

MARY
(Shouting)

Mr. Barnum, I don't believe wolves dislike killing.

BARNUM
(To Mary)

I beg your pardon?

MARY

You said wolves don't like killing. I don't believe it.

BARNUM

I didn't say they don't like killing. I said they don't like smelling.

DIANA

Hula-hoop . . .

OOSKY

Mr. Barnum, your clearly implied that the root of the flower of ethics springs from some physiological contradiction. That may be so, so far as your wolves are concerned. *Our* ethics, however, *human* ethics, begin with a Revelation, which is as it should be. Because without a revelation, nothing is really ever intellectual. Without a revelation, everything turns in solipsist hula-hoops, round and round and round . . .

(He demonstrates)

DIANA
(Provokingly)

And *with* . . . ?

JOHN
(Promptly)

And *with* a revelation, everything is straight and straight and straight, like a . . . Ha ha ha!

MARY
(Gaily)

John! That's the first time I've ever heard you laugh!

DIANA

What a happy sight! Look, John is laughing!

OOSKY

You are not an atheist, John! I hope . . .

JOHN

Don't be frightened of atheists, Mr. Oosky. Your arch adversary is the devil, not the atheist. And he could not afford to be an atheist. He would lose his raison d'être.

OOSKY

The Devil is not an atheist. But atheism is his work.

MARY

What do you think about Love, Mr. Barnum? Have you ever considered . . .

DIANA

Leave Mr. Barnum alone, Mary. He must be allowed a quiet moment to think about his beautiful wife, and his child who is playing with her hula-hoop.

STEVE

He didn't say his wife was beautiful.

MARY

. . . have you ever considered Love as the basic concept, the golden key for the understanding of the Universe?

DIANA

What a bore you are.

MARY

Let *him* answer.

DIANA

Good manners are more important than Love. I'm sure Mr. Barnum would prefer to be left alone by a wolf who hates his smell, than be killed by a Christian who loves his soul.

OOSKY

Such preference may be acceptable as a matter of expediency. Not as a principle. Love is divine. Therefore ethics without God . . .

JOHN

If Mr. Barnum's theory is correct, and the origin of all our ethics is the conflict between our need for flesh and our dislike of its decomposed smell, then your enemies, Mr. Oosky, are called not 'atheists' but 'deodorisers'! Remove the smell of death, and the foundation of ethics vanishes into thin air. Ha ha ha!

BARNUM

(Who has ignored Mary's oration, moves towards John and repeats his last words)

Precisely! Just as you said, "Remove the smell of death!" Ladies and gentlemen! An air of putrefaction encircles us. Whether we are aware of it or not, it enters our nostrils and plays havoc with our nervous system. Do you think it is a coincidence that all the great religions were born in warm countries, where the anaerobic process of decomposing proteins is quick, and the effect enormous? No. It isn't a coincidence. The Kings of Egypt tried to embalm their bodies, the funeral pyres of India oxidized them in the flames, grave-diggers hurried to bury the proteins in graves, medical men kept them in formalin, cooks salted them, boiled them, braised them, grilled them, invented a hundred methods of keeping the odour of death away from the nutritive cells, but it is still hovering around us.

(He sniffs)

Don't I feel the smell of a dead bird in this house? Does it not ooze into this room and poison your mind, your feelings, your life? And it is so easy to get rid of it irrevocably. Ladies and gentlemen!

(He lifts, or points to the white case)

Here is a really effective, reliable and compact piece of modern equipment designed to produce and utilise both sound energy and refrigeration for the disintegration of contamination and disruption of micro-organisms, lysis of red blood corpuscles, depolymerisation of molecules, dispersion of solid and liquid particles – you put your bird in, and the breeze of death is removed from it instantly and for ever. Ladies and gentlemen, this is a portable (I have carried it myself in one hand), ultra-sonic disintegrator-cum-refrigerator. And this, ladies and gentlemen,

(He points to the black case)

is an equally portable, self-contained, constant feed-back temperature-controlled deep-wave cooker, browning your decontaminated, death-free sustenance from the very inside . . .

JOHN

(Turning to him wildly)

Shut up.

Mr. Barnum is never out of his depth. He scrutinizes the others, one by one.

DIANA
(Half-dreamily, to herself)

Mink coat . . . hula-hoop . . .

STEVE

Good show, Mr. Barnum.

OOSKY

I should like to see you helping us at the Church Bazaar, Mr. Barnum.

MARY

I think you are sweet, Mr. Barnum. You know, a short while ago I wanted to ask you to take your shoe off.

They look at her enquiringly.

MARY

To see whether he hasn't got a cloven hoof, you sillies.

DIANA
(To herself)

Hula-hoop and mink coat.
(To Mr. Barnum)

Does your wife really dream of having a mink coat?

BARNUM

Oh no. She isn't as foolish as that.

DIANA

How does she dress?

STEVE

Mr. Barnum, what do you think of the future of the world?

BARNUM

(Scrutinizes Diana from the top to toe)

She dresses exactly like you do.

(Pause)

I didn't tell you that before, because . . .

DIANA

Never mind why you didn't tell me. Mr. Barnum, you are a marvellous salesman, and I . . .

STEVE

Mr. Barnum, would you consider becoming our public relations officer? You must have heard about our group.

DIANA

Steve, haven't I been asking you, since you were one year old, not to interrupt me when I am busy? I am discussing business with Mr. Barnum. I am in possession of something which I am confident Mr. Barnum will be able to sell for me at a considerable profit.

(Mr. Barnum is speechless. Diana turns to him:)

Mr. Barnum, I offer you a commission of 20%, provided it is sold at or above the price it cost at the time it was manufactured, taking into consideration the devaluation of the pound during the last 20 years, and . . .

MARY

(With suspicion)

What are you going to sell?

DIANA

I am going to sell your father's coffin.

BARNUM

(Stupified)

A coffin? Is your husband dead?

DIANA

Of course not, Mr. Barnum. How can you? The coffin is quite empty. You will see it in a moment.
                    (She goes to the wall and rings the bell)
It is heavily built, approximately your size, quite decent, no silly ornaments . . .

JOHN

Diana, you can't sell Daddy's coffin, you simply can't!

DIANA

It is not I, it is Mr. Barnum who is going to sell it for me, John. And there is no reason for you . . .
(She notices the parlour maid who has just entered by the door on the
left)
Peggy, please go to my bedroom and bring your master's coffin. Mr. Barnum wishes to see it.

PEGGY

(Unconcerned)

Did you say: coffin, Madam?

DIANA

Yes, Peggy. Ask Nelson to help you.

PEGGY

Very well, Madam.

(Exit)

STEVE

And what will Daddy do if you sell his coffin and he has to pronounce another sentence of guilty?

DIANA

He will have to spend the night in my bed instead. And it may do his soul a lot of good, Steve.

(Turning to Mr. Barnum)

You may not know, Mr. Barnum, that my husband is a hopelessly moral man, who insists on paying his debts. Psychological debts. He hasn't any others. And so, whenever the jury's verdict obliges him to put on the black cap and pronounce the usual formula, he comes here and spends the night in his coffin. These are about the only occasions when he comes home. When you come to think of it, we do not see him here very often . . . Fortunately! . . . or unfortunately?

(Reflectively)

You know, Mr. Barnum, sometimes I feel like one of your howling wolves, I feel the stress of two contradictory directives, and become quite hysterical about it. I want my husband to come home, and at the same time I *don't* want him to come home. I want him to come because I can't stand the sight of the empty coffin. And at the same time I dread his coming, because he snores, and it is grotesque to see a judge snoring in a coffin when each sound reminds you that at that very moment, somewhere, in a prison, there is a man, a criminal, who is going to be hanged by the neck until he is dead.

BARNUM

(Overcome)

Mrs. ffahrenheit, I . . .

(He was going to say that he would do his best, but he stops suddenly, as if forcing himself out of a spell)

What the devil! I came here to sell, not to buy! A coffin! You were pulling my leg, Madam.

DIANA

(Promptly)

Were you with your hula-hoop?

BARNUM

(Startled)

Hula-hoop?

DIANA

Hula-hoop!

BARNUM

(Rapidly)

I am not selling any hula-hoops! I am giving you a unique chance of acquiring a portable ultrasonic disintegrator-cum-refrigerator and an equally portable diathermic short wave deep-penetration cooker and baker.

JOHN

(Turning on him, firmly)

We are not interested.

BARNUM

(Attacking)

Neither am I!

JOHN

(Taken aback)

You sounded as if you were . . .

BARNUM

(Energetically)

Nonsense, my dear sir. I don't care a damn. Why should I? They bore me to death. They make me feel sick. Why should I be interested in these pitiful gadgets wherein the marvels of modern science have been dishonoured by being applied to trivial domestic purposes? I am interested in orders, not in cookers! Give me your order, sir, and you may do with these two boxes whatever you wish.

(He kicks the boxes. He takes two sheets of paper out of his pocket and a fountain pen)

The boxes are of no importance, Sign these two orders, and you can throw the boxes out of the window.

JOHN

(With determination)

All right.

(He signs one of the papers)

Mr. Barnum gives him the second paper.

JOHN

(After having signed the other paper)

And now help me to throw them out of the window.

John lifts the white box and gestures to Mr. Barnum to lift the other. They do to the left window. Without hesitating John throws his box out. Howling voices outside. But John has already taken the black box from Mr. Barnum's hands and thrown it too. At the same moment Steve, who is sitting on the balcony, opposite the window, gives a shout. But it is too late.

STEVE
(As indicated above)

Stop it, John.

Long dead silence. Steve jumps up, rushes along the gallery, down the stairs, and disappears through the door on the right. After a moment Diana approaches the window, looks out, takes a step backwards covers her face with her hands, then crosses the stage and goes out through the same door. The others follow her, all except Mr. Barnum.

At this moment the door on the left opens and Peggy, the parlour maid, enters, followed by Nelson, both carrying the coffin. They look round, puzzled at seeing the hall empty; they take no notice of Mr. Barnum. They put the coffin down, parallel to the footlights, right under the chandelier. Peggy goes to the window on the left and shuts it, without looking out. Puzzled, they exit through the door on the right. Mr. Barnum crosses the stage towards the piano. He has to go round the coffin. He stands at the piano. Sits down on the piano stool. Turns round. He takes the two sheets of paper out of his breast pocket, looks at the signatures, and puts them back again. He turns on the piano stool in the opposite direction. He strikes one note on the piano; he takes a sandwich out of his side pocket. Unwraps it. Has a bite. He puts the sandwich on top of the piano. He crosses the stage and disappears through the door on the left. After a moment he comes back carrying a glass of water, obviously taken from the bathroom, in his right hand and, absentmindedly, a toothbrush in his left. When he is in the middle of the room, going towards the piano, the maid appears hurriedly through the door on the right, rushing towards the door on the left. She notices, however, the glass of water in Mr. Barnum's hand, snatches it from him and runs out through the door on the right. Mr. Barnum approaches the piano, puts the toothbrush by the side of the sandwich. Takes the sandwich and sits down, but gets up immediately, puts the sandwich back on top of the piano, crosses the stage, disappears through the door on the left and, after a moment, comes back carrying another glass of water in his right hand and another toothbrush in his left. He puts the toothbrush on top of the piano, picks up the sandwich, sits down, has another bite. Drinks some water.

He gets up, puts the sandwich and the glass on top of the piano.

He walks upstage, looks at the portrait of the Judge handing on the wall there. Looks out the window, looks at the portrait again. While he is doing that, the maid and Nelson come in through the door on the right, take the coffin and carry it out through the same door.

Mr. Barnum turns round, stops at the place where the coffin was, goes to the piano, sits on the piano stool, turns round. Takes the two sheets of paper out of his breast pocket, refolds them differently, and puts them back again. He turns on the stool in the opposite direction, then, with one finger, tries a few notes. He plays them almost staccato, with very long pauses between the notes.

Through the door on the right, John appears, in a state of utter despair, running in and across the stage towards the door on the left, through which he disappears. Mr. Barnum gets up, undecided. He stands *under the chandelier, goes back to the piano, takes another bite of the sandwich and a sip of water. Puts the sandwich and glass back on top of the piano, sits down and waits.*

The clock strikes one.

SCENE THREE

Through the door on the right the "cortege" enters. Mr. Oosky and Steve in front, Nelson and the chauffeur at the back, carrying the coffin on their shoulders. Mary walks on one side, Diana on the other. Peggy, with a large parcel in brown paper in her arms, follows.

In the coffin the Judge sits stiffly, his chin haughtily lifted, implacable. He holds a stick with a gold knob in his right hand.

JUDGE
So that is how I am received in my own home.
(Pause)
And the photographers will be here any minute now.

DIANA
Photographers? To do what?

JUDGE
To photograph.
(Pause)
To take a picture of me resting serenely in the bosom of my family, and publish it in the glossy magazines you read in Harley Street.
(Pause. He touches Mr. Oosky's shoulder with his stick.)
It is all your doing, Mr. Oosky.

OOSKY

(Astonished, but he cannot possibly turn round because of the coffin he is carrying)

My doing, Sir?

JUDGE

In the Civil Service Hierarchy, the Cabinet Minister who sits at the top of the ladder is responsible for the clerk who makes a nuisance of himself at its foot. I understand that in your establishment, it is the footstool that is responsible for the headgear.

OOSKY

It may be so, though I have never thought about it. Do you mean to say, Sir, that I am responsible for the Archbishop?

JUDGE

I do. You are.

OOSKY

Well, I am sorry, Sir. And I should like to know what he has done.

JUDGE

He found it to be his pastoral duty to tell the Prime Minister that according to certain information which had been brought to his attention, I had not spent a night in my country home for almost two years, which fact, according to him, is damaging to my reputation. Well, I could hardly tell the Prime Minister that I see my wife every first Sunday after Hilary, after Easter, after Trinity, and after Michaelmas at a Brighton hotel, which is nearer, and where we are far more comfortable than here.

MARY

Oh, Father!

JUDGE

(To the coffin bearers)

Try to keep still, if you can.

MARY

(To Diana)

Oh, Diana!

DIANA

(To the Judge)

Let me call the doctor, please Cecil.

MARY

(To the Judge)

Oh, I am so happy! I am so happy!

JUDGE

We are all glad that you feel happy, Mary, and would like to know why.

DIANA

Wouldn't you be more comfortable if they put you down on the floor, Cecil? You must feel giddy up there.

JUDGE

I am perfectly comfortable as I am, Diana. I enjoy this position, which gives me a new view of the whole situation.

MARY

Oh, Daddy!

JUDGE

(Admonitorily)

Mary!

MARY

Oh, Father! . . .

STEVE

Diana doesn't like us to call her Mother, and Father doesn't like us to call him Dad.

JUDGE

I do not see any inconsistency in that, Sir. Do you?

STEVE

I don't know. I suppose there isn't any, Father.

OOSKY

I hope you didn't mean to say, Sir, that I have been providing the Archbishop with information concerning your private life.

JUDGE

Certainly not, Mr. Oosky. Certainly not. I know that you are incapable of doing anything that could better your position in this world.

(To Mary)

I believe, Mary, you wished to tell us why you feel happy.

MARY

(Candidly)

I feel happy, Father, because you said you had come home to be photographed. Because I had been thinking that you had come as you used to, Father, because you had condemned a man and wanted to . . .

JUDGE

(To Diana, stiffly)

Diana.

DIANA

Yes, Cecil.

JUDGE

I thought it was tacitly understood between us that that subject was not to be discussed in this house, ever. Since she was a little girl, Mary has been forbidden to make any mention of it. Has she not?

DIANA

She is no longer a little girl, Cecil.

MARY

I resent being talked about as if I were miles away. All I said was . . .

JUDGE

You misinterpreted what I told you. I said that photographers were coming to photograph me. I did not say I came to be photographed. I have come to celebrate.

(To Diana)

Did you remember that today is our silver anniversary?

DIANA

Yes, I read about it in The Times this morning.

JUDGE

Dear old Times. Always there with the news on the breakfast table.

OOSKY

(Without turning his head)

Congratulations, Sir. All my best wishes, Diana.

DIANA

Thank you.

OOSKY

't' all right.

JUDGE

If you open the parcel I have brought, you will find something in it that I hoped might please you.

(The maid takes the parcel over to Diana)

I am sorry if it looks a little as if it has been trampled on by a mad elephant, but when the first incredible box fell from the window and shattered my big toe, I showed, I think, great presence of mind by putting the parcel on my head and thus protecting it from the second. I must confess that that rainfall of boxes still remains a mystery to me.

DIANA

(Who has opened the parcel)

A mink coat!

(She holds the coat in front of her and will put it on presently)

BARNUM
(Who, unseen by the Judge, has all this time been standing by the piano)
A mink coat! Ha!

JUDGE
Who is that?
> *(To Mr. Oosky and Steve, touching them with his stick)*
Turn round, please, gentlemen. Turn round.

The coffin turns round so that the Judge can now face Mr. Barnum.

JUDGE
(Calmly)
Are you one of my wife's lovers, Sir.

BARNUM
Not at all, Sir, I'm afraid . . .

JUDGE
(Interrupting)
I do not wish to hear any details.

BARNUM
I have none to . . .

JUDGE
(Noticing the sandwich on top of the piano)
You shouldn't let her feed you on sandwiches. You should ask for a

proper meal. It is luncheon time, is it not? May I see the glass, if you don't mind.

Mr. Barnum passes the glass to him. He sniffs at it and gives it back.

JUDGE

Water! How absurd! And unexpected, Mr. . . .

BARNUM

Barnum is the name, Joshua Hieronymous Barnum. A travelling salesman who has just chanced to pay his first visit here this morning, if it pleases your Lordship.

JUDGE

Mr. Barnum, I am "my Lordship" only for criminals . . . and barristers.
                    (He chuckles)
For my friends I am Mr. ffahrenheit.

BARNUM

Sir, you force me to disclose that I am Mr. Barnum only for my clients. For my friends I am Mr. Straker.

JUDGE

(After having searched in his memory)
Straker, Sir? The name sounds familiar . . .

BARNUM

I believe it might . . .

DIANA

Cecil, I insist on sending for the doctor. The mink coat might have protected your head, but your big toe was black and swollen . . .

JUDGE
(Ignoring her)
You are not . . . What was the name? . . . *David* Straker?

BARNUM
No. How could I be? Unless I were his ghost.

DIANA
Mr. Barnum, I apologise for not having offered you any whiskey or asked you to share our meal with us, but as you see . . .

BARNUM
(Ignoring her)
He died two years ago. As you may remember.

JUDGE
Are you . . . a relative . . . Mr. Barnum?

BARNUM
That is so, your Lordship.

JUDGE
I asked you not to address me thus, Mr. Barnum.

BARNUM
I'm sorry. But you see, I have been addressing you that way so many times in my dreams . . .

MARY

(Her voice is very strong and clear; there is an authority in it; it cannot be ignored)

What were you saying to my father in your dreams, Mr. Barnum?

BARNUM

Night after night, asleep or in sleepless dreams, all through the long trial, I knelt again and again in front of your berobed and bewigged father, saying: "Why do you not believe him, My Lord? I *am* my brother's keeper, My Lord, and I know that he is innocent. You see, My Lord, don't you, every word he says condemns him and brings him nearer to his grave, but it is because he is innocent that he says them, an imbecile, but an innocent, who does not see where blind adherence to the truth is leading him. If you believe him when he condemns himself, My Lord, why do you not believe him when he says that he is innocent?"

(Pause)

That was, more or less, what I was saying to your father whenever he came into my dreams, Miss ffahrenheit.

Silence.

JUDGE

Mr. Barnum, would I be right if I were to say that your presence here is not due to pure coincidence?

BARNUM

I think you would be right if you were to say that, Sir.

JUDGE

Perhaps you may judge that I am entitled to know what its purpose is?

BARNUM

A river rises not in order to make a breach in its banks, but because too much water has accumulated in it. What has accumulated in me can be called, I think, . . .

(He looks for a word)

– curiosity.

JUDGE

Pray continue.

DIANA

Please, Cecil, you can't ask them to carry that weight any longer.

The Judge lifts his hand to silence her.

DIANA

And I think we should ask the doctor to come . . .

JUDGE

(Ignoring her)

You said: curiosity.

BARNUM

Curiosity! Yes, curiosity. I wanted to know, to see with my own eyes, how he looks, without his robe and wig, in the privacy of his home, the man who killed David Straker.

JUDGE

I will not allow that expression in this c . . .

(He coughs)

It seems to me strange that you do not know the working of the law. The man in question was found guilty by the jury. When that is done, there remains nothing for the judge but the formality of putting the black cap on his head and pronouncing the sentence. After which, the course of justice proceeds along the road provided for it by the law of the land.

BARNUM

And the word "killing" is not used. You cannot pin it on to anybody's clothes. Neither to the Sunday jackets of the twelve gentlemen of the jury, who are told to answer only one question: Guilty, or Not Guilty, nor to your ermine into which you retract like a snail into its shell, nor to the apron of the executioner who is nothing more than the final prolongation of this anonymous mechanism. My goodness! I am glad I came. Look – what a picture!

(He points to the coffin)

What a picture!

JUDGE

If your curiosity is now satisfied, Mr. Barnum . . .

STEVE

Mr. Barnum, you're a fine guy!

JUDGE

Steve, *I* am talking to Mr. Barnum.

STEVE

With your permission, Father, I wanted to ask Mr. Barnum whether he has also visited the jurymen . . .

BARNUM

I have. I have visited 10 gentlemen of the jury in their homes. The remaining two unfortunately happened to die in the meantime.

STEVE

And . . . ?

BARNUM

I sold them seven refrigerators, five vacuum cleaners, one kitchen table, one electric fan and two washing machines.

STEVE

Good show!

BARNUM

Life must go on, you know!

DIANA

Steve, keep still. You'll make your Father seasick if you go on fidgeting.

MARY

(Who has been crumpling a bit of brown paper in her hands, tears it in two)

Mr. Barnum, if you say another word, I shall scream! I asked you before, but you weren't listening. Did you never consider Love as the key that solves all problems . . .

DIANA

(She is in her mink coat now)

Be careful, Mary. Love is a wild animal that must be kept on a lead.

And a very complicated lead it is. It must be short enough to allow the butcher to kill the lamb, but it must be long enough to prevent us from destroying each other.

BARNUM

I agree, Madam.

JUDGE

Mr. Barnum, I was saying that if your curiosity is now satisfied, we shall take leave of you and proceed.

BARNUM

There is still one thing I should like to know.

JUDGE

Yes?

BARNUM
(Slowly)

Where is John?

JUDGE

John? Who is John?

BARNUM

Your son, John.
(He strikes one note on the piano)

DIANA

John! Where is John!

MARY

John!

Mary and Diana exit. Mr. Barnum exits. The coffin moves off. The Judge looks at the chandelier as they pass under it. Then he stops the bearers.

JUDGE

Stop for a moment, will you. Go back two paces. I knew there was something wrong with that chandelier. Look, the chain isn't on the hook. All it is hanging on is two thin electric wires. It must be put right at once. Will you see to it, Nelson?

NELSON

Yes Sir.

JUDGE

Then let us move.

The coffin moves slowly towards the opening on the left, through which they disappear. The maid collects the brown paper, the gun that was left under the window, then Diana's riding breeches and jacket that were left on the armchair and, loaded with all these she goes out through the door on the left.

The stage is empty for a full 10 seconds. The chandelier falls down with a bang.

Curtain

LECTURES

Themerson 57.

THE CIRCLE OF ART
AND SCIENCE*

I have just come from a place where I spent the weekend in the company of some forty scientists, forty worried scientists, anxiously trying to find out who she really is, she, the Muse to whom they have consecrated their lives.

As six of the scientists I am talking about are members of this Common Room, I must ask their forgiveness for this baroque way of referring to the Second Conference of the Philosophy of Science Group, which has just taken place at Nottingham.

For me it was a very valuable experience. The only thing I regret is that because of the conference I happened to miss the exhibition of pictures painted by the two monkeys Mr. Francis N. Souza was so amusingly telling us about the other Thursday. However, I must at once tell Mr. Souza that if he had gone to Nottingham he would have learned one or two things capable of giving still more anxiety and embarrassment to the members of his profession.

He would have learned, for instance, that Dr. Ross Ashby, of Gloucester, is busy building an electromagnetic machine which will

*These thoughts on the Second Conference of the Philosophy of Science Group, held in Nottingham in 1957, were presented as a talk at the Gaberbocchus Common Room, September 26, 1957. Mr. Themerson is author of *Bayamus* (1949), *The Adventures of Peddy Bottom* (1951), *Wooff, Wooff, or Who Killed Richard Wagner* (1951), *Professor Mmaa's Lecture* (1953), *Factor T* (1956), *Kurt Schwitters in England* (1958). The Gaberbocchus Common Room (associated with Gaberbocchus Press, Ltd.) is at 42A Formosa Street, London W.9. It combines the functions of reading room (magazines from many countries, including *ETC.*), meeting place, chess room, and restaurant. Thursday nights are "Gaberbocchus At Home," when there is usually a film show, a recital, or a talk.

draw all sorts of lines, and will do so not for any practical purpose but, so to speak, for its esthetic pleasure.

Dr. Ross Ashby is a young, I think, man, with a long grey beard. And he has built a number of ingenious devices which perceive, classify and memorize information, and act accordingly, just like human beings do. Now, so far as I understand his intentions, Dr. Ashby does not aim at building a complete human analogue. On the contrary – I understand that if he builds machines which imitate as many human activities as possible, he does it in order to see how far one can go in that direction, when one will have to stop, and what it will be that remains and cannot be imitated. Whether that final thing will be what makes Dr. Ashby Dr. Ashby, or what makes Souza Souza, we don't know. It may be that Dr. Ashby hopes that nothing will remain, but he doesn't say so.

However, it is not only painters who may find anxiety – or inspiration? – in experiments of that kind. If a *maître de ballet* had visited Nottingham, he would certainly have pricked up his ears at a bit of news about the trick Dr. Grey Walter played on one of his mechanical tortoises. You have heard about his tortoises, who walk where they like, see each other, and, when they are hungry, go to an electric point and plug themselves in. Now the story goes that Dr. Grey Walter took one of his tortoises and put it in front of a mirror, and the tortoise's photoelectric eyes lit up like those of a debutante at the moment the ballroom door opens, its little wheels trembled, and the tortoise started a war dance, making all the typical gestures described in the works of anthropologists.

However, it is not the hypothetical uneasiness of artists or dancers that I want to talk about. No. There were no artists at Nottingham. There were forty worried scientists, trying to find out what it was all about, and looking embarrassed, or, let us say, puzzled. Perhaps they were not aware of it, perhaps they will object, perhaps there were some exceptions – anyway, that was how they looked to me, extremely, deeply, puzzled, by realizing that the world consists of some events which may be noticed, observed, examined, predicted, brought into being, and all that *not* by scientific methods. What kind of events? Well, even their being puzzled was one of such events. As you can guess, it was the old problem of dichotomy again, yes, but in a rather specific version. As if something new had suddenly crept in. What was it? Well, before I am more precise about it I would like to say something else.

A little while ago there was a fashion which consisted of dividing the world into events that could be detected, and events that could not be detected. The first – putting it simply – was thought to be the domain of science; the second, the domain of religion. Logical analysis, however, has convinced at least some of us that to talk about the existence of something that cannot be detected is neither true nor false, but just devoid of meaning. It is, as they say, like talking about a cat who cannot be seen, heard or touched: a cat whom you may call, but who will never put in an appearance. Having thus, through logical analysis, and with the help of Occam's razor, shaved away the invisible cat of religion, it was thought, for a moment, that all the visible cats that remained were measurable, experimentable-with, predictable, etc., and therefore belonged to the domain of science. And, in general, it is so. You can measure their whiskers, and the result is relevant to what we mean by a little, domesticated, pet tiger.

There exists however a strange, perplexing, exotic strain of perfectly visible cats which, nevertheless, cannot be satisfactorily dealt with by scientific methods. I mean, you can measure their whiskers, but the result, correct as it may be, has nothing to do with the animals. You can count their teeth, or analyze a sample of their tissue, and you know perfectly well that the results, though verifiable, have absolutely nothing to do with what those cats are about.

I think you have already guessed that the visible and audible animals I am talking about belong to the class in which you can find such physical objects as rectangular bits of canvas covered with some stuff which has optical properties, which rectangles some people call pictures, or such series as certain temporal configurations of acoustic vibrations, which some people call music, or even such events as that embarrassment experienced by the forty scientists, which some people call a state of mind.

The cat is visible, it doesn't disappear into thin air, and yet what we find out about it by following the electric pushes in its nerves does not seem to be relevant to its smile.

What an embarrassing situation!

Signs of that fundamental embarrassment were shown, now and again, at Nottingham. Why else should Dr. Mary Hesse, when talking on "Observation and Experiment," finally say that something or other in mathematics was not like translating from one language into another, but like translating from poetry into prose? Was not Mr. Ron F. J. Withers puzzled by the difficulty of knowing which patterns of canals, which networks in a biological preparation (I don't remember its name), belonged to a tissue which was being examined, and which were what he called "artifacts," superimposed on the preparation by the technique used by the experimenter? What are those "artifacts" he was talking about? I would like to see them. *Artificial facts superimposed on bits of life carved out of the natural world!* Doesn't this sound dangerously near to a definition that could be applied to many things that we call pictures, or poems? What an embarrassing thought for both the scientist and the artist!

Professor J. H. Woodger must have been aware of this embarrassment, as he decided to do something to clarify this somewhat new version of the eternal mind-versus-body confusion. Bravely enough, he started by assuming what he called "epistemological innocence." "Tom leaned out of the window and got a view of the sea," he said, and seemed puzzled by the fact that a sentence like that can communicate some knowledge to another human being. Trying to find out why that was so, he suggested dividing the world into three classes, of which the first would contain the "getters," "doers" and "talkers" – I would simplify that here by saying "persons." The second class would be the class of perceptions, and the third class of – let's say crudely – physical objects. The third class, he said, was the domain of science. Of course. The second class, that of perceptions – was it not, he asked, the domain of artists, such as painters and musicians? And the first class, that of persons – getters, doers and talkers – was that not the domain of literature? What an extraordinary thing to happen – the name of art, the name of literature – mentioned alongside the name of science! It was as if somebody might have said: "At the time of Wellington there lived, across the channel, a general of the name of Napoleon Bonaparte."

By being rather flippant at this point I don't mean to say that science without art and literature would be nothing, or that art and literature, without science, would have conquered the universe. I think the whole trichotomous division is, at best, arbitrary. I'm sure that Professor Gilbert Ryle thought there were too many classes in it, but Professor Ryle sat there smoking his pipe and not saying a word. It is true that his book, in which he exorcized the ghost out of the machine, was not mentioned. Neither was Russell's magic to get rid of the dichotomy by discussing the world in terms of events and not in terms of things. It is perhaps characteristic of assumed innocence – not only in epistemology – that it gives you a kick forward, but at the same time leads to greater confusion. I hope this need not necessarily apply to unassumed innocence. I hope so, because it is that that I intend to display now.

When writing this page, I told myself: "Now I will shut my eyes for twenty seconds, and then I will open them and see what questions will force themselves up in my mind." And I shut my eyes, and then open them, and the questions were: Where am I? What is it all about? What is it all for?

Well, where am I? What is it all about? What is it all for? Is it significant that I must inhale a cloud of tobacco smoke to answer this question? Well, here I am, September, 1957, London, England, the sky, and some kind of geometry behind it. Here am I, and there is the world, past, present and future, and the distance between *here* and *there* depends on mood. Sometimes it is miles and miles and the world recedes; sometimes it is zero, and the world creeps into the very cells of my body, leaving nothing for myself. It all depends on mood. But it is not a philosophy of mood that I intend to display here. It is quite possible to be maneuvered into a mood in which a particular statement seems to be obviously true. Neither am I a solipsist. I wouldn't be here if I were one, though even that is not entirely correct. Nor do I wish to talk about existence. After all, you are, therefore I think. And, after all again, sometimes I am *more* aware of your existence than of my own. But all this is only to indicate on which level of abstraction I want to discuss the problem: What is it all about?

What is it all about, that science and art dichotomy? Here is a human being, whom we call an artist, and there is the whole world around him. And here is a human being, whom we call a scientist, and there is the whole world around him. This is the first, simple, almost-not-worth mentioning, fundamental similarity. However, there is a difference. And that difference will be our point of departure. Here is an artist surrounded by the whole world, and there is a scientist surrounded by the whole world. But the world that surrounds the artist contains in itself the scientist. While the world that surrounds the scientist contains in itself the artist. What happened at Nottingham was that scientists became aware of there being an artist in the world that surrounds them. Of his being there, not independently, not alongside the scientists, but in their universe of discourse.

The theologian, looking for invisible cats, used to stand along-side the scientists, didn't belong to their universe, and could there-fore be dismissed, or dealt with in the department of psychology. The artist, however, deals with visible cats, belong to the scientists' universe of discourse, and cannot be dismissed or transferred.

What is happening outside of Nottingham is that artists are becoming aware of there being a scientist in the world that surrounds them. Not alongside, but *in* the world. In formalizing these statements, I do not advance any particular theory. They are not propositions. They are subjects for investigation. However, before we attempt that, we must break those generalizations, *art, science.* As if they were two monolithic armies, each composed of identical, mass-produced brains and souls, aims and abilities. There is as much difference between a Hieronymus Bosch and Marilyn Monroe and Hugo Manning, as there is between Tycho Brahe, Norbert Wiener and Dr. Hutten. What have a Praxiteles and a Charles Chaplin, Henri Rousseau and Schoenberg, Marinetti and J. S. Bach, T. S. Eliot and Ulanova – what is it that they have in common, and that makes us call them all *artists?* And what is it that Euclid and Madame Curie, Lobaczewski and Thomas Alva Edison or, let's say Poincaré and J. B. S. Haldane – what do they have in common that makes us call them by the one name of *scientist?*

Definitions of *science* are many; they vary from one level of abstraction to another, shedding, as they climb up, their causations, predictions, and verifiabilities one after another, ending perhaps in some such frivolous formulation as: "the production of useful tautologies."

Definitions of *art* are also many, all terribly arbitrary, irrelevant, incongruous, moody, incoherent. Do you really think that Picasso would be lost in the deep forest of long molecules, or among the traces left in the Wilson Cloud Chamber? Or do you think that Heisenberg could not conduct an orchestra? Ladies and gentlemen, if you happen to have identical twins, for heaven's sake let one of them become scientist and the other an artist, and when they are at the top of their careers, bring them to this Common Room and show us the result of your experiment.

Through a green park of Nottingham University I walked one evening with a scientist who told me that it was the artist in him that made him become a physicist. It was the artist in him who felt the urge to find, in the maze of this world, something that would be perfectly clear, non-equivocal, something that would make sense, even if only within its own framework, something that would possess the beauty of being simple and straightforward. Physics, he said, theoretical physics, is the only thing that can provide him with this.

I venture to suggest that this physicist would have more in common with Johann Sebastian Bach, or Mondrian, than with another scientist, one who is anxious and impatient, fascinated by the thought of what will happen if he puts two things together, combines molecules, builds fantastic, unpredictable structures of electronic circuits, and watches sharply and pitilessly the result of his fever. And is not this last-mentioned scientist more like a Dadaist, a Kurt Schwitters, who put odd bits together, odd bits of what had belonged to different units, and was fascinated by thus creating something new from pure relationships?

And what about the biologist, investigating a slice of living tissue, obsessed by it, coloring it, cutting it, observing, experimenting, building in himself a picture of what is and what is not important in it, and then selecting and describing what is significant in it, carefully putting down all the details with passion and obstinacy – is he not like Emile Zola? Or he who invents psychological, sociological, political hypotheses, yet cannot make laboratory experiments elsewhere than in his own imagination, and writes a novel or a play – is he not like a theoretical physicist, or like a Newton, who could no more push a real planet out of its orbit to see what would happen than Shakespeare could push the real Ophelia into the stream? They both built in imagination. And the only *checkability,* in both cases, is that what is unknown must be consistent with what is known. That the imagined hypothesis must be consistent with tangible details. In the case of scientific theory, we say it is consistent. In the case of a Shakespeare or an Agatha Christie, we say it is convincing. There are many mansions in the houses of both artists and scientists.

It would be very strange if it were a coincidence that, when the world surrounding the artist became filled with the shapes of objects displaying straight lines, sharp edges, definite, machine-made forms, that, at the same time, the artist invented cubism. It would be very strange if it were a coincidence that, when line liberated itself in the artist's picture and began to appear on paper or on canvas in its own right, that at the same time, lines, graphs, dots, statistical curves started to fill the pages of scientific journals. It is not only that the *landscape* we both live in, changes, gets filled with aeroplanes, Woolworths, photographs and signboards. We come to realize that scientific *words* and *shapes* are not emotionally neutral: that scientific tools increase our vision without asking us to give up our esthetic emotions. The insertion of the Mount Wilson telescope between the poet's eye and the Milky Way no longer makes the sky less lyrical for him. As medieval travelers used to come back from foreign lands with their stories of strangely shaped creatures and fill the sculptor's imagination with visions, the results of which crowd the walls of Notre Dame de Paris and other Gothic cathedrals, so scientists come to us today with their X-ray and infra-red micro- and ultra-micro-snapshots, ready to build visions in our reluctant imaginations.

Yet, this is not all. It seems that science supplies us not only with the sight of things that have never been seen before, but also with new patterns, constellations, relevances, that have never been thought before, and with phenomena and manifestations that have never existed before. Science enables us to see the puzzle of the world, not only in terms of things – with the soul, or soulless – but also in terms of intervals, or in terms of events. Is this the origin of the striking similarity that can be observed between the new shapes that are in the vocabulary that science uses in her endeavor to discover or to say something significant about the world, or to add something to it – and those shapes we encounter in what we call modern art?

There is something more than coincidence in it. As if something essential, straight from the bowels of the universe, were in both. Next Thursday, Dr. Calvert is going to show us some sculptures which are, in fact, mathematical models, representing equations. Some time ago they were seen only as mathematical models – today, as you will see, they are sculptures. Something has already happened. It is not a question of dichotomy, or trichotomy, as Professor Woodger suggested. On the contrary. There is some kind of unity in the whole process.

Science locates physical stimuli and physical reactions in physical space. It was felt, however, that this was not all, that this was not enough. It was inferred, therefore, that there must be something else, somewhere there, as well. Hence the dichotomy. But there may be nothing else there.

And so my point is *not* that something else, somewhere there, may exist, but that something else about the same thing can be said. It is the artist who feels that he has something to say about it, that he has gained some knowledge, not about that something else, but about the same physical stimuli and physical reactions that happen in physical space, but knowledge which he cannot express by using terms taken from the scientific vocabulary. Anxiously he gropes around, looking for tools, for means of communication, putting physical shapes or sounds together so that they can model not so much a bit of reality, as the bit of *knowledge* he has gained. And this trying of his, this activity of his – is art (or, at least, one aspect of art). Thus, if we agree that (at least in some cases) what an artist has, and wants to communicate, is knowledge, then the next question is: can it be verified?

Now, what is that business of verification like? A scientist observes some events (or referents), then he forms some thoughts (or references), then he tells them to himself and to others by putting together a number of symbols (which may be words, signs or graphs). Then, if you want to verify his statements, you can take the set of symbols he has put together in a certain pattern, and compare them with the events that he observed, which you can re-evoke in your laboratory.

For an artist, the first two stages seem to be the same as those of the scientist. He experiences events, he produces some thoughts, he puts together a number of signs to express them, but when *you* want to verify them, to put them alongside the primary events that the artist has experienced, you may find that they are no longer evokable, and that they are in some inaccessible place *in* the artist himself. And the only thing you can do is to compare the set of signs with the memory of events which are not in him, but in you yourself.

Now, if his events and your events are entirely different, if they have not a single member in common, the set of signs (a work of art), will be entirely incomprehensible to you. If, however, the proportion of similar things to dissimilar is such that, understanding the similar ones, you can, as with a half-solved crossword puzzle, decipher the others, then you gain knowledge that has been acquired for you through his, and not through your, experiences.

Modern science has penetrated modern art as medieval science penetrated medieval art. And as medieval art was pushing and pulling medieval science, whatever she was, so does modern art with modern science. Because, after all, when all is said and done, scientists find only what they are looking for. And they are looking for one thing and not another, and their imagination works one way and not another, and their imagination works one way and not another because their mind has been shaped that way by the poetry they read, and the pictures they look at, and the music they listen to.

And thus art and science become inescapably interlocked, and the circle is closed.

GEOMETRY OF SATIRE

Satire and Civil Liberties – this is our subject. It consists of three elements: the first is Civil Liberties; the second is Satire; and the third – is *us*! I see us as living within a system of co-ordinates; they are historical co-ordinates, geographical co-ordinates, and cultural co-ordinates. They are never the same, never identical for two different people, but also never entirely different. It may be this flexibility that makes a man a reed, but at the same time it may well be his tenacity that makes him a thinking reed.

Us. Without co-ordinates, without a system of classification, whatever that may be, there is chaos. Our eyes see nothing, our ears hear nothing except white noise; it may well be that only our noses that lead us to the breasts of our mothers, towards the perfume of our lovers and away from our biological enemies.

The co-ordinates – or, if you like, the system of classification – represent the first step that lets us out of our zoological cage. Unfortunately, the same step takes us into another cage. The bars of this cage are the co-ordinates put there by our brains – the cage of the philosophical system. It aids our efforts to examine the universe. It also gives us a feeling of security, it protects us against that which goes on outside it. Yes, it is a nice cage of mental security. Provided that we don't believe that it is the only possible cage. From the moment we start believing that it is the only possible cage, we transform enlightenment into obscurantism.

*

Philosophers debate: are all swans white? They call that a problem of induction. In other words the question is: should we verify the truth or falsify the hypothesis? Demonstrate that all swans are white, or that we can't find any black ones? (There are black swans in Australia but Australia is too far away from Oxford or Cambridge for anyone to take black feathers seriously.)

Then all of a sudden a Gentleman arrives, a Gentleman who isn't necessarily a philosopher; he turns a green spotlight on to some swans and shows us that they are all green, I call this gentleman a Humorist. And if another Gentleman arrived and showed us that it is the light of the spotlight that is not absolute, that it could be red, for example, I would call him a Satirist.

A Humorist is someone who takes an object out of one cage, transports it into another, and hey presto!, what we thought was **A** has become **B**. And yet our Humorist hasn't in the least changed **A**. He has merely transported it into another system of classification.

And that's precisely what we do. We throw objects from one cage into another, and if we demonstrate that what seemed to be a Pegasus becomes a peccary when we throw it into a different cage, people call us humorists. And if during this operation we destroy the cage itself, they call us satirists. But we are humorists or satirists despite ourselves. If you want to be a satirist don't try to be a satirist. Try to look for the truth. In fact if we look for the truth, we almost automatically become a satirist. For satire is in the world, and not in us satirists.

*

When a general or an archbishop steps on a banana skin and falls over, we want to laugh. This event has transported him from one cage to another, and we now see that he isn't merely a general or an archbishop but also a human being. Immediately, all the cultural baggage we carry ready-made in our brains in preparation for this meeting with the general or the archbishop is no longer necessary, and we feel we have dispensed with it. And this sensation of being liberated is accompanied by what we call laughter. What had been the truth when the general or the archbishop was on his feet stopped being the truth when the banana skin made them fall over. We have made a discovery, namely that truth is not absolute, that it has its own valid domain. And we don't need to wash our hands like the old hypocrite two thousand years ago when he asked: "What is truth?"

And sometimes this discovery can tell us quite a few things about life. It was not a writer who has caused us to make this discovery. It was not a poet who made the general trip. It was a banana skin – life itself. So perhaps it is life itself that is at the same time the humorist and the satirist.

*

A few years ago I was talking to some Polish writer friends and they asked me: "Do you know why we Polish writers don't have absolute liberty? It is because the authorities think too highly of us. They think that what we write is so important that they can't allow us complete freedom. They think that it is the poets who can, like a banana skin, make the generals fall.

In England, the situation is certainly very different. There, one can write whatever one wants. Why? Because the authorities don't bother with such things. They don't think that what one writes can have the slightest influence on present-day politics. So they leave their writers absolutely free. There, the satirist can write whatever he likes because he doesn't count.

With the journalists, it is not quite the same. They count. And in consequence, their freedom is not without limits. Of course there is no censorship. That's true. But there are other perfectly legitimate ways of encouraging prudence. For instance, one can give them information and ask them not to use it in their articles. And they don't use it. This is called playing the game. If poets are free because they don't count, and journalists because they play the game, it seems that the only liberty worth fighting for is that of printing four-letter words.

*

We mustn't think that the satire is always directed against "the biggest battalions". No. I remember having seen in Paris in 1940, an issue of *Der Stürmer*. This little magazine, I recall, satirized the shape of the nose of people who were condemned to death. The satirist succeeded in transferring the object to which he was paying attention from one cage to another in such a way that for those who inhabited the same cage as himself, the shape of the nose became the sufficient reason, almost the Supreme Reason, for destroying not only the object that possessed it (a human), but also the system of co-ordinates – philosophical, sociological, etc. that previously protected him.

Satire, then, is not always on our side. "Our?" But who are we? "Men of good will?" That is not a definition, it is a desire. If you can define the "our" satisfactorily, in such a way that your definition includes us all, wherever we happen to be, in no matter what country, belonging to no matter what political party, simultaneously excluding all the "others" – (I'll leave it to you to define the "others"!), if you can do all that, well then, do it! Your definition will be the foundation of a spiritual edifice of enormous importance. A great sociological and philosophical System. A cage of the most delightful co-ordinates. I hope that the bars of this marvellous cage will be sufficiently close together so as to prevent the "others" from penetrating inside and at the same time far enough apart so that I myself can escape.

*

Allow me to return to our banana skin, with its miraculous power to transport a general or an archbishop from one system of co-ordinates to another.

I propose to call the first of these systems *"the cage of established co-ordinates"*, and the other *"the cage of unmasking co-ordinates"*. I suggest that it is the transportation from the established cage to the unmasking cage that makes us laugh. Yet if you were to look around carefully, you would find people who were not laughing. It would be too easy just to say that they have no sense of humour. It's quite possible that they would find it quite amusing if it had been one of "us" who had fallen stepping on a banana skin. Which means that humour is not absolute either. But what is it, then, that makes people react differently? It seems to me that it is their attitude to the cage of the established co-ordinates. There are some people that the cage of the established co-ordinates does not naturally suit, and even if they accept it, it is in spite of themselves. It weighs heavily on their shoulders and its bars limit their freedom. But there are others who accept it, who believe in it, who cannot imagine life other than in the cage of the established co-ordinates.

Obviously, "the banana effect" will be different for those two groups. The people in the first group will feel that they have suddenly been liberated from a system which oppressed them. The others will feel disorientated.

The shock of unexpected liberation, the muscles relaxing – all this is manifested in what we call *laughter*.

But the other shock, the shock of derailment, is a drama.

And in the case when the general and the archbishop fall so heavily that it is not only their behinds that are damaged but also the *whole established cage,* that will be a satire for the first group and a tragedy for the second.

*

The systems I have just described seems to me to be valid not only for those going downstairs to find a banana skin awaiting them at the bottom, but also for those going upstairs.

If a child dresses up in an army or ecclesiastical uniform and pretends to be a very important personage, it makes us laugh. The passage from one system to another is easy.

On the other hand, if the same thing is done by Gogol's Government Inspector, or if it's a German cobbler, Wilhelm Voigt, who dresses in the uniform of a Prussian army captain and becomes the Captain of Köpenick, the system itself trembles, and this event becomes a satirical event.

Two thousand years ago, a man of humble origin proclaimed himself King. Naturally he said that his kingdom was not of this world, but there were some satirists around who put a crown on his bloodstained head and threw a royal cloak over his stooped shoulders. But years went by, and history changed the meaning of this satirical gesture.

History takes revenge if people mock those who represent the unmasking system. One wonders whether the formula is the same when the revealing system appears to be reactionary? I think so. For example: It was very difficult to satirise Hitler before he came to power, and that not only because he wasn't evil enough, but because he was opposed to the established system of co-ordinates.

The formula seems to be the same whatever the reality in question. The satire of the Copernican system could seem quite amusing to the Ptolemeans. But it didn't survive. The satire of the Ptolemean system is still valid even though it doesn't amuse us any more.

It isn't altogether the same with Newton and Einstein. Einstein wasn't trying to replace the system of the Newtonian co-ordinates by a new system. What he put forward is a formula that is valid for every imaginable system. And that is something completely different. Einstein's relativity marks the end of all systems; therefore it's the end of laughter. Since if all systems of co-ordinates are relatively equal, a banana skin can no longer transport us from the established system into the unmasking system. So this is the end of humour and satire as we have known them until today. Perhaps it also marks the beginning of what one calls 'black humour'.

*

If you will bear with me, I shall tell you a little story. A story about something that happened to me last night, here in Conegliano. I came by train. It was raining. I was carrying my bags and was looking for somewhere to leave them, when a Gentleman in a very beautiful uniform addressed me. I didn't understand a word of what he said and I thought that he wanted to help me. That wasn't the case. Another Gentleman appeared and told me in French that the Gentleman in uniform wanted me to open my bags. I asked him why. He explained the Gentleman in uniform wanted to verify one of his scientific hypotheses. A hypothesis that I had some plastic bombs in my bags. I answered that I had come to Conegliano for a Satirical Conference and not for a Plastic Conference; nevertheless, as he insisted, I allowed him to verify his hypothesis; or rather, to refute it.

This little incident made me ponder. And I came to the conclusion that one of my civil liberties is not to be bombed plastically or otherwise.

So if the Gentleman in uniform opens my bags, it is he who is the defender of my civil liberties – and perhaps a more efficient defender than satire is. This paradoxical thought amazed me. You see, satire doesn't accept any absolute god. It isn't absolute. It satirises and must be satirized. And if I have told you this little story it isn't to satirise the Gentleman in uniform but to satirise satire.

Translated from the French
by Barbara Wright

THE CHAIR OF DECENCY

I am greatly honoured in being asked to address you and to give this Johan Huizinga Lecture, and I hope you will agree with me in thinking that he, who taught us that the subject of Cultural History is not History but Culture, would find congenial to him the two theses which I'm going to submit to you for your consideration.

Means rather than Aims

The first thesis, putting it simply, asserts that Means are of greater importance than Aims.

Gentleness— biological; Aggression— cultural

The second asserts, that, contrary to what clergymen and policemen want us to believe, Gentleness is biological and Aggression is cultural, not vice versa.

These are two ways we can take to arrive at such conclusions:

a scholarly way – by employing analysis, discussion, argumentation;

and a meandering way – by living a very long time and letting our experiences do the mental work for us.

As my age has become much more impressive than my scholarship, I have chosen to voyage with you along the latter, the meandering way.

*

History
&
physics
or
Faites tirer vos gens!
&
the Leyden bottle

Let me begin by confessing that when I first heard the name of your noble university, as a young schoolboy, some 60 years ago and miles away Eastwards, it was not in connection with your great historian, but in association with the physicist (P. van Musschenbrock) who in 1745 invented the so called Leyden bottle.

1745 was the year when the famous phrase *'Après vous, messieurs les Anglais'* originated, and the word 'pragmatic' referred to the army defeated at Fontenoy, not having yet become a philosophical term meaning that our doctrinarian assertions are to be judged by their consequences.

My schoolboyish notion of chivalry made me quite impressed by these phrases exchanged between Lord Hay and le Comte d'Auteroche: *'Faites tirer vos gens!', 'Non, monsieur! à vous l'honneur!'* – but the Leyden bottle was infinitely more fascinating. Just imagine: an empty marmalade jar; you coat it with tin foil, within and without; you connect the inside with an electric friction machine, and then, later on, hey presto! you approach your finger – and a flash of lightning!

Who would have predicted at the time that the Road of Political History, on which the battle of Fontenoy was an episode, on which the Leyden bottle was also an episode, would become so entangled with each other that we should again hear the familiar words: *'Faites jeter vos bombes, messieurs les Russes!', 'Après vous, messieurs les Américains!', 'Non, messieurs! à vous l'honneur!'*

*

We yearn for metaphors, models, parables, that would help us to understand. We long for analogies, though we know that to argue by analogy is liable to produce false conclusions from true premises. Because analogies are misleading. Not only historical analogies.

Analogies mislead

Imagine two identical pieces of ice: one floating on the surface of the river Styx, the other on the river Scamander. The similarity of the situation may tempt us to draw one and the same conclusion. And yet, one piece of ice may be in the process of growing, because the temperature is falling, while the other piece of ice may be in the process of melting, because the temperature is rising. The example looks trivial, but it won't look so trivial if, instead of comparing two identical pieces of ice in two rivers, you compare, say, two identical numbers of prisoners, not necessarily political, in two countries of which one is moving up, and the other down, on the road of progress, or freedom, or reason, which is probably one and the same road.

As little history as possible

To know the direction of the movement, we must, of course, have history. But we need not as much of it as possible but as little of it as possible. It is the momentum, the vectorial quantity of the present fraction of a second that tells us where the aircraft is going to. The history of its yesterday's meanderings confuses our judgment. Can History really explain how it happened that we find ourselves where we are today, with so much dirt on the heels of our shoes and so much blood on our hands?

'*Fautes jeter vos bombes!*', '*Non, messieurs! à vous l'honneur!*' It isn't even clear: do they calculate how many of their bombs to throw on each other, or on us, who are in between?

*

Human size & Human understanding

Once upon a time, we used to help our understanding of the world by reducing (or enlarging) everything to Human Size. By human size I mean things bigger than a flea and smaller than an elephant; history longer than the duration of a single flap of the wings of a moth and shorter than a century; weights heavier than a petal falling down from a cherry tree and lighter than the burden Atlas held up on his shoulders.

There we are: the CGS system of Classical Physics.

Egyptian Gods, and Greek Gods, and Roman Gods, were of human size. And Jesus also chose to be born of human size, so that it would be easier for us to understand His way of dealing with the enormity of the Tragic factor contained in the edifice built by His Father.

Today, things are the other way round. Today, all our poor human-size phenomena are being explained to us by reference to things very big, such as galactic dust, primordial soup, the Big Bang (which reduces our Cosmos from something necessary, fundamental, to a mere historical, contingent event), or else they are explained by reference to things very small: molecules, chains of DNA, atoms, quarks . . . all those things that are proved by experiment but unknown to experience — unless you'll say that proving something by experiment, even an imaginary experiment, is an experience.

*

Experiments & experiences

A scientist counts some figures, he finds that the proportion of little white mice that have survived, or not survived the experiment, is significant, and he smiles as he goes to the canteen to have his cup of tea.

A writer finds the right word and the right place to put it in the right sentence, and a smile appears on his face.

A little peeing-boy lifts up his little penis, and when the liquid parabola hits the target, his eyes brighten with pleasure. Or else, he sulks because of some disappointment. Or cries because he has hurt his thumb.

These are simple experiments and experiences. But there are some others which don't produce laughter, or sulking, or cries of pain.

The little boy holds in both hands a big box of chocolates. But he is not interested in the contents of the box. He is interested in its lid. Because on it, *The very small* there is a picture of a pretty lady who is holding in her hands a box of chocolates on the lid of which there is a picture of a pretty lady holding in her hands a miniature box of chocolates on the lid of which . . . The boy's eyes cannot come any closer, his seeing processes cannot go any further, but his thinking processes can. Now, if he comes to the conclusion that there is no end to the series of pretty ladies holding boxes of chocolates, maybe, one day, he'll become an axiomatic mathematician, or a dogmatic politician . . . ? On the other hand, if he thinks there must necessarily be somewhere there the very tiniest, ultimate pretty lady whom you can't reduce any further, maybe he'll become a physicist, or a novelist . . . ?

The very big But now he looks up and notices above the portal of the Cathedral a bronze semi-circular high-

relief, in the middle of which sits the Holy Mother
of God, holding in her hands a model of the whole
Cathedral, above the portal of which . . . No, this time
he doesn't try to look 'inwards'. This time his mind
moves outwards and make him imagine a huge,
invisible Mother of God holding in her hands the *real*
Cathedral, and then, a bigger still, bigger than the
sky, Mother of God holding in her hands . . . There
he stops. Either his intuition has told him that the
whole thing is becoming ridiculous in the way only
grown-ups can appreciate, or else, perhaps . . . Who
can know? Perhaps the very biggest, the ultimate
Mother of God is, by some conjuring trick, a hocus-
pocus which only grown-ups can explain, the same
person as the tiniest pretty lady with the box of
chocolates . . . ? He tries a piece of chocolate, and his
mind has already dismissed the very big and the very
small, and gone back to the human-size imaginary
experiences: a comic strip, Nat Pinkerton detective
stories, Pitigrilly's naughty phantasies? Things are
again natural, intelligible, and simple. But then he
meets some Great Masters who want to clarify his

a Great
Confusion
thoughts, and everything becomes a Great Confusion.

*

The adventures
of an imaginary
schoolboy in his
search for a
philosopher-king
The first of the Great Masters whom our imaginary
schoolboy met was a man called Plato who, over
2000 years ago, in a discussion with his intellectual
friends, expressed the view that the troubles of
mankind will not end till true philosophers are given

political powers and become rulers of states. As our imaginary schoolboy was well aware of the troubles of mankind, and wished them to cease, he decided to undertake a search for a philosopher true enough to be a good replacement for Mrs Thatcher, Mr Reagan, and the like. It so happened that the first philosopher he met in his noble search, was one of the Natural Philosophers, nowadays called Scientists.

Scientists?

The world of the Scientist's mind was sandwiched between two worlds: the outside world, and the world of the blackboard on which some mathematical white squiggles were chalked. The Scientist was very conscientiously trying to achieve a sort of aesthetic, pretty, one-to-one relationship between the patterns he chalked on the blackboard and the patterns he was able to discern in the world. Meanwhile, the Mathematician who stood at the Scientist's elbow, watched jealously that the pattern on the blackboard would form by itself an independent, consistent set, free of contradictions. This conscientious, striving after some concordance between the FORMS produced on the blackboard and the REALITY of the world, pleased our imaginary schoolboy so much that he was already willing to suggest a Scientist-cum-Mathematician as the replacement for the political rulers . . . Alas, the very next day, he met in a tramcar his professor of chemistry, attired this time in the full regalia of the military uniform of Major-general, and learned that the subject of the professor's researches was poison gas.

Painters? Disheartened by this discovery, he turned from the Scientist's laboratory to the Painter's studio. The world of the Painter's mind was also sandwiched between two worlds: the outside world and the world of the canvas covered with paint on which various shapes and colours began to appear. Some were referring to the outside world, some others to the inner world of the Painter, and some others still to the inner world of the canvas itself. All this pleased our imaginary schoolboy very much, but when, the very next morning, he learned that the very same Painter had gone to an art gallery and there assassinated the very first President of a republic that had just achieved its independence, he, the imaginary schoolboy, decided that *that* method of replacing political rulers by members of the thinking classes was perhaps not what Plato would advocate.

Confused by his experiences, our imaginary schoolboy came to think that perhaps Confusion is a necessary, immanent part of all Human Understanding, and so he directed his steps to where the Confusion was the greatest, he went to see Philosophers. Great Philosophers.

Philosophers? The trouble with great philosophers is that each great philosopher tends to define things in his own idiosyncratic way. Because a really great philosopher would never accept another really great philosopher's definition of a philosophical term. It seems even that the very greatness of a really great philosopher consists in giving a different meaning to a term used by other mortals, philosophers or not.

There was, however, one among them who was not only a great philosopher but also a great man, who cared 'for what is noble, for what is beautiful, for what is gentle. Who saw in imagination the society that is to be created, where individuals grow freely, and where hate and greed and envy die because there is nothing to nourish them.' And so, at last, our imaginary schoolboy thought that he had already arrived at the end of his search for the platonic philosopher-king, -president, or – at least – -prime minister, when – and it happened late in the year of our Lord 1948 – the Philosopher came to a *logical* conclusion that the United States should threaten an immediate nuclear war on Russia for the purpose of forcing nuclear disarmament upon her. This statement was so unexpected that the Philosopher himself soon forgot that he made it – so out of harmony with his past and future thoughts and deeds, for which he and his wife went to prison in the country that claims to have no political prisoners. And the schoolboy's affection for the man hadn't suffered, but he was dismayed by the logic that treated global issues as if they were arithmetical facts represented by signs in the system that could be manipulated as if they had no meaning, the logic in which there were no symbols representing ordinary

Symbolic logic
&
ordinary lives

lives of ordinary people who are neither dissidents nor war-mongers, and want to marry, or divorce, have children, or not, play the balalaika, drink a glass of vodka, listen to Yevtushenko, or go to a cinema, just like some other ordinary people, on the other side of the Ocean, want to marry, or divorce, have children, or not, play a guitar, drink coca cola, listen to Frank Sinatra, watch advertisements on television, or have the luxury of dying in one's bed.

Democracy (?) So, perhaps, after all, Plato was not quite right when he said: 'If the democracy of Athens had consisted only of educated persons, no fatal harm would have been done.' Perhaps the very essence of Democracy stems from the fact that the proportion of wise to stupid, good to bad, rational to tempestuous, is the same, whether you search among philosophers or priests, poets or peasants, politicians or generals, economists or dockers in the shipyards of Gdańsk.
I don't know.

Ways of seeing the world

There are two ways of seeing the ways of seeing the world. One is one way, and the other is another. And nobody knows: 'Is there, anywhere, one way of seeing the two?' This is neither a statement nor a question. It is an expression of a kind of feeling. Have you ever had that feeling? It made me put aside all my books and the newspapers, made me switch off the radio,

The aims of aims

made me go to a park and sit on a bench and reflect, made me walk through the streets and reflect, made me lie on my couch and reflect, and the reflection, both melancholy and not sad, was like the hand of a watch, moving round and round and round, always forward, and always coming back to its point of departure. Hence melancholy: because questioning the essence of progress.

I wanted to grow a crystal, and bring it to you as a gift. I wanted to wrap it nicely in words, and give it to you tonight. Alas . . . and it is not that I'm not capable of putting forms in symmetries of rhymes and rhythms . . . but crystals grow from undisturbed tranquility, and this I couldn't find in myself.

Thus, I got up from my bench, stopped in the middle of the traffic, jumped out of my dream: What I shall bring you is a flaming torch, a loudhailer, an *Allons, Citoyens!* Fortunately . . . and it is not that I'm not capable of putting rhymes and rhythms into a howling cry . . . but, having lived through hairpin bends of History, and met and seen and heard some howling voices, both true and false (the former is more dangerous), I called my sense of humour to stop me, just in time.

Thus, I have come to you tonight empty-handed, having no offerings of Aims to give, because no Aim is so exalted that it be worth a heartbeat more than Decency of Means. Because, when all is said and done, Decency of Means *is* the Aim of Aims.

*

Some naïve lovers of semantics believe that if only our rulers, our saviours (of all sorts), could understand the meaning of their own pronouncements, they would amend their ways. What an illusion! They, the saviours, know the mechanism of Language much better than all the Semanticists, Linguistic philosophers, and Logical formalists put together. That's how they know how to use it to play upon the prejudices of the mob: you and me.

Poetry
&
Politics

And, when a Poet, or a Novelist, becomes a Demagogue, the same applies to him. Because POETRY, as well as POLITICS, may be morally *vicious*, and intellectually *dishonest*. In such cases, both poetry and oratory – political, religious, philosophical – are like crime. The greater a crime is, the more impressive it is, but the less excusable.

Thus, when all is said and done, one finds that no poetic rhymes, no greatness, no philosophical systems, no reasons of state, no politic ends, and no utopian aims are more important than decency of means. Because, when all is said and done, decency of means is the aim of aims.

*

'formalism is the
opium of the
thinking classes'
(Allan Calder)

And here, straight from the lopped and barked wood of bare trunks, come some classical formalists, who dream their dream about the world of distinct nouns and predicates, governed by the yes-or-no law of the excluded middle, the world in which things (including you and me and him and her) are what they are, and are not what they are not. And they dream their dreams to their logical conclusions, which are true in all possible worlds, except the world in which we live. Because in the world in which we live, no noun is timeless, no predicate makes sense without the rest of the universe, no fact is what it is and nothing else, and no man is an island. And when we feel not at our ease in their dream, they say: 'You must believe us, because our assumptions are good, and our logic is true, and if you don't see it working, it's because our dreams have never been tried.'

Which is not so. All dreams have been tried. All have worked, partly. And all have *not* worked partly. And they *did not* work whenever their sires and seers, and the successors of the sires and seers, believed that if their assumptions are good, and their logic is true, then the conclusions become aims, and all methods can be used to achieve them; that the end justifies the means.

The end
&
the means

In this, their faultless formal axiomatic logic omits two facts:

ONE: that in this changing world, the way from premises to conclusions is temporal and stormy, and you can't force your Yesterday upon your grandson's Tomorrow;

TWO: Oh dear . . . Well . . . Yes, it has been said in the Sermon on the Mount:

'But I say unto you, That you resist no evil: but whosoever shall smite thee on thy right cheek, turn to him the other also.'

It is a saintly thing to turn and offer your other cheek to be slapped. You can do it once. You can do it again. You can do it thrice. Perhaps. But when the thing goes on, and your persecutor doesn't relent, and the thing becomes a method, left cheek, right cheek, left, right, left, right, left, right, all saintliness disappears, and what remains becomes either a low farce, not good enough for Charlie Chaplin, Buster Keaton, Max Linder, or Laurel and Hardy, or else it has to be stopped. Often by force. Which, invariably, becomes vicious itself. And hence a tragedy. Because we can't do anything about it. There do exist tragic situations when wicked means have to be used to suppress some other wicked means that are already with us, but to use wicked means to promote aims – defeats the aims. The Crucifixion defeated the aims of the chief priests and the scribes and the mob and the Establishment and the Empire; The Inquisition dehumanized the aims of Christianity; The Labour Camps degenerated the aims of Socialism. For millions of people, Socialism was the continuation of Christianity by other means. And it was the viciousness of the means that had poisoned the decency of its aims.

Socialism: continuation of Christianity by other means

*

'Naturalistic fallacy'

Now, let us not get ourselves sidetracked by academic questions: How to define what is not definable by definition: how to define 'wicked' and how to define 'decent'. As if we didn't know what we mean when we use these words, however differently we use them. As if the reality of the emotive and commanding force that is in us was less real than the confused reality of things to which these unanalysable undefinabilities refer. Thus, whatever your notions of the wicked and of the decent are, whatever is the practical use you make of them, the wickedness of your means will destroy your aims, even if those aims are good only for some group, class, faith, race or nation, and to the detriment of all the rest of us, because all wickedness destroys all decency, and even for the wickedest logician the aim of aims is some sort of decency of means.

*

On Decency

'Decency'! What an embarrassing word! You have to brace yourself to pronounce it. But I couldn't find a better one. If you want to refer to something wicked, vicious, offensive, aggressive, you have a hundred words to choose from, and people show confidence in you, they assume that you know what you are talking about. But if you brave it out and use the word 'decent', they think you are a sissy, a nincompoop. Johan Huizinga knew that characteristic of our age.

'Pretence of vice'

He called it 'Pretence of vice'. In his essay *The Task of Cultural History*, published in 1929, he regarded it as

(from: *Men & Ideas*
translated by
J.S. Holmes &
Hans van Marie)

'a modern repetition of the sentimentalism of the eighteenth century, but in a completely different form. The old sentimentalism,' he wrote, 'felt itself to be intimately bound to the respect of virtue. It tended to balance passion and virtue in what was often a neck-breaking fashion. Nowadays this is no longer necessary. Passion alone, or what figures for it, is enough. In every depiction of reality in either word or image . . . the element of passion must be played up. Moral norms definitely may not be praised. Virtuous people assure themselves of their halo of the modern by means of a eulogy of immorality. Such a eulogy is as much a form of cultural hypocrisy as a sanctimonious display of virtue was ever able to be.'

And, we can add, it is still more acute today than it was when he wrote about it. That's why, I must confess, I felt as if I were actually displaying some sort of courage when I decided to use the word 'decency' in a straightforward way.

What sort of courage?

Dogcatchers

When I was a small boy, one early morning on my way to school, I met a gang of dogcatchers. A sordid big wooden box on wheels, pulled by a blind horse, at the back of the big box a little barred window through which you saw a pack of stray dogs, already caught and condemned to death, except for a bitch in heat who seduced them there. The dogcatchers were four in number. Three were for rounding up while the fourth was armed with a long stick at the end of which there was a short rope with a slipknot, like a lasso. He was just ready to lift it to catch a stray brown mongrel, when I, the little schoolboy, put my little foot deliberately into the centre of the loop, knowing perfectly well how the brutes, the ruffians, would curse, and jeer, and laugh, and make fun of it. Why is it so that today, as soon as I decided to use the word 'decency', I had the same feeling, the feeling of putting my foot deliberately into the loop of a lasso?

*

Flower Children

What the word 'decency' stands for is not only laughed at, it is also held up to scorn and derision. Do you remember the Flower Children? Young people, dressed with flowers and bells, proclaiming Flower Power, and carrying flowers as symbols of universal peace and love, not aware perhaps of how much hatred had been created in the world in the name of love! I feel as if I saw them yesterday, but it was nearly twenty years ago, in the sixties. One night, at about that time, I was sitting in a pub, on the corner of Randolph Avenue and Warrington Crescent, slowly sipping my whisky, when a man of my age took the seat beside me and started a conversation by saying how awful the new generation is. 'Oh yes . . .' I said. You see, in France you start by saying 'Mais, *non!*,' even if you agree with what has been said. In England you start by saying 'O yes . . .' even if you disagree. You say 'Oh yes but . . .' So I said: 'Oh yes, but do you know what happened to me yesterday? I was walking with my wife along the Edgware Road when we saw some young people, four boys and two girls, marching in a row in our direction. When they were a step or two in front of us, we stopped, not without some apprehension, and they stopped, and gave us a bunch of flowers. Upon which they quietly went their way.' As I said that, the man in the pub, the man of my age, put down his glass of beer, and said . . . Well, do you know what he said? He said: 'How disgusting!'

*

Second thesis

I have been meandering for so long around that Cinderella word 'decency', because I need it. I need it for my Second thesis: that gentleness is biological and aggression is cultural, not vice versa. In other words, that, in general, people don't like to be murderers, unless it is for the sake of an idea.

Let me at once make it clear that I am not going to talk about Ethics. I'm not going to talk about Ethics because I'm not interested in Ethics. And I'm not interested in Ethics because I'm interested in what Ethics is about. You see, this is not a paradox. I am interested in what Ethics is about, but She is not. She, the academic Goddess of Ethics, is interested only in herself. I am interested in ethical behaviour,

Ethics & ethical phenomena; discovered & invented

but she is interested only in ethical terminology. For the last eighty years she's been sharpening her linguistic tools, but she thinks it would be unladylike to use them. So let me leave her and her tools to her academic Robinson Crusoe insularity, and go back to what one would expect to be, but isn't her subject matter, namely ethical phenomena.

The trouble with ethical phenomena is that some of them are discovered and some of them are invented. Those we have invented didn't exist before, and we may call them Cultural Ethical Phenomena. It's easy to point out some of them: The Ten Commandments, Code Napoléon, Principles of Literary Criticism, or Police Regulations. But what about those which *did* exist before, and which we may call Biological Ethical Phenomena? Have there really been any? Do we have any proofs of their existence? Well . . . My

I am the proof

very presence here, in front of you, is the proof.

Now, I beseech you, do please take what I'm saying in the literal sense of the words, without allegory or

The fact that your mothers haven't eaten you is remarkable; don't take it as a matter of course

metaphor. I repeat, my very presence here in front of you is the proof. The proof that when I was small and defenceless, my mother didn't eat me, even when she was very hungry. And your very presence here is the proof that your mothers haven't eaten you. And you will agree with me that they didn't eat us *not* because of some clergyman or policeman who might or might not have exhorted them not to. And the lioness also wasn't in the habit of eating her cubs millions of years before she devoured a Christian who could have taught her the Lesson. She not only wouldn't eat them, she would lick them with all the gentleness of her red, rough, stinking tongue. That's why I said in the first half of my thesis that gentleness is biological. It is biological in the strict genetic sense. It is both genetic and ethical. What a pity that philosophers put Nature and Ethics in two different compartments. There is no reason why we should call 'ethical' only that normative kind of behaviour of our brain structure which answers to *do! don't! must! ought! good! bad!* given by a divine or civic authority, and not to that triggered by hormones or pheromones. The latter, the genetic demeanour, is much stronger and of greater significance. It is this that makes the survival of the species possible.

Gentleness is both biological & ethical

Hormones & pheromones are also emotive & commanding

Young boys and girls are taught that unfortunate Darwinian expression 'the survival of the fittest', and they imagine a strong muscular male, a Muhammad Ali, or a Tarzan, Grrrh! But the prodigious strength of Cassius Clay was preceded by the gentleness of his mother, and the chivalresque strength of Tarzan by the gentleness of the female African Ape who brought him up. So perhaps *The survival of the gentlest* is more to the point. Because when the gentleness disappears through mutations, or through some cultural factors, as might still happen to men, the extinction of the species is inevitable.

The survival of the gentlest

It is a pity that the truth about Original Virtue, the

virtue of biological gentleness, has been engulfed in our lore by the cultural invention of Original Sin, the

Tragic Necessity is in Nature, Evil is in Culture (for more about 'Tragic Necessity' see: *factor T*, by S.T., London 1956)

sin of natural evil. There is Tragic Necessity, but no natural-evil, in the man who kills for food. And there is no natural evil in the lioness who kills her Christians. All the evil is in the culture of the Emperor who has sent them on to the sands of the arena. Maybe that's how their faith survived that of the Emperor. Because it was he who used vicious means. They, so far as I know, were still innocent plebeian crusaders, not taking other people's lives, not sending letter-bombs by post, not planting time-bombs in the tabernae, shooting at a quadriga, or hijacking a sea-going triemis. It's curious that I understand those simple lovers of God better than I understand that sophisticated lover of Art, the art of happenings, the Roman Emperor Nero. Though I am not a believer.

On the contrary, I am too-oo religious, if you see what I mean, to believe in anything, if you see what I mean; not even in the Linguistics, if you see what I mean, of the anti-mystics, if you see what I mean; because I'm too religious, to believe in anything, if you see what I mean.

*

Original Sin
&
Original Virtue

Original Virtue excuses no man. Original Sin does. Original Sin is a pretext for pessimism; Original Virtue is not. We have studied Original Sin for ages and preached it as the deprivation of Grace involving Guilt, and as the source of all ordinary sins and miseries. But the study of the Original Virtue of gentleness and of the consequent ordinary virtues of common decencies has been most neglected. And yet, the phenomenon itself exists, and has enough virility and reality to claim as a right its place in philosophy, science, and public life. Should we not study it as we do other demonstrable though invisible things? Should we not create a Chair of Decency at our Universities? A chair of the Physics of Decency and of the Molecular Chemistry of Gentleness? A Department of Altruism? A Faculty of Kindness? A Kinsey Report on unselfish behaviour in human male and female? A Research Institute for the studies of structural differences in the mechanics of inter-governmental good manners?

The Chair of Decency

Some people who refuse to take notice of the Original Virtue of Gentleness and prefer to believe in the Original Sin of Evil, are of the opinion that we would all be committing all the actual sins, all the time, on all occasions, were it not for two reasons: The first is voiced by the clergyman who tells us that there is a system of rewards after death; the second by the policeman who reminds us that there is a system of punishments on earth. It is regrettable that no serious academic research has been done on the practicality of these two systems. Or, if it has, that it hasn't become common knowledge.

On clergymen & policemen

The only piece of research I saw on the first subject, was

a badly documented report saying that at a certain time at a certain place there was a proportionally greater number of Roman Catholics than of Unbelievers among those who had been convicted in the criminal courts. To which Msgr Gavarni said: 'All statistics lie'. Msgr Zorge said: 'Frogs commit still less crimes than Unbelievers, so what?' Msgr Liutprand said: 'To commit a crime, you've got to have guts, and catholics have guts'. And a little Franciscan brother hanged himself in his cell. As scientific research, surely not enough to generalise upon.

(see: *Cardinal Pölätüo*, London 1961, but see also a report by Clifford Longley, Religious Affairs Correspondent of *The Times,* 15.9.1981)

Nor have we anything like a Kinsey Report on the second subject. The Police. All we have is opinions and exclamations, silences and screams. Even from their own professionals.

(*The Times.* 27.8.1981)

'I don't give a damn for the bleeding hearts, the so-called liberals and marxist agitators who can do nothing but complain about police brutality', says Mr James Jardine, Chairman of the Police Federation. 'Police *are* political in any society', says Ms Irene Wilson, a Staff Tutor at the Police Staff College, 'both as individuals and as an occupational group'. 'The police attracts conservative and authoritarian personalities', explains Detective Chief Inspector Gorman.

(*The Times.* 25.10.1981)

But hark! Here is Chief Inspector Butler. He doesn't think opinions are enough. He advocates academic research into policemen's attitudes of mind. 'There is an unfortunate lack of academic research on the police,' he says, 'such research should be encouraged.' Thus, as I am a *practical man*, it occurred to me that, perhaps, it might be a good and practical idea to elect to our academic Chair of Decency not an Oxford Moral Philosopher, preoccupied with such problems as . . . I quote literally: Whether from *This is good* you can always infer *Therefore choose it*, for instance *This is good chocolate* therefore *Take it*, which, in ethical context, becomes *Let everyone take it*, but, rather, the Chief Inspector who is familiar with what's going on behind the Closed Doors of a police station, and has personal knowledge of cruelties committed in the name of Justice, cruelties committed in the name of Charity, and cruelties committed for their own sake.

Whom to elect to the Chair of Decency?

Well, I don't know . . . Our attitude towards police is most ambiguous, equivocal, confused . . . Once upon a time, before the atomic age, a sergeant in the army would give a lesson of patriotism to a conscript by putting to him this standard rhetorical question: 'Wouldn't you defend your sister if a man was trying to rape her?' This psychological trick didn't work with only one man who was a pimp and whose sister was a well known whore, but otherwise it must have been effective because it was used in the armies of many countries. In peace time, the question will rather be: 'Wouldn't you call a policeman?'

'Wouldn't you defend your sister ... ?'

We all avoid the policeman when we are breaking the law, but we expect him to be within call when a lawbreaker attacks us. And yet, when we see a policeman marching a handcuffed man, green with fear, not into a cage in the zoo, where we could observe what was happening, but behind the Closed Doors of the police station, our feelings are confused, to say the least. We don't like the closed doors behind which one person is in the power of another, whether it's a police station, a prison, or a mental home. Our thoughts vacillate. Though I once met a young man whose thoughts didn't vacillate at all. He knew exactly what to do, and did it in his own unusual way.

He was neither a criminal, nor a victim of persecution, nor a victim of his own thirst for power, but it just so happened that he had had a few pints of beer and, late one night, when walking in the streets of London, he felt a sudden urge to empty his bladder. As everything was closed, he turned to a narrow side-street, stood in a niche in front of a padlocked door, and unzipped, or unbuttoned, when a heavy hand fell on his shoulder. Two policemen were standing behind him. The shock was such that his vesical sphincter contracted and he was unable to demonstrate his reasons for being where he was, upon which he was accused of trying to 'break and enter'. After spending the night in the police station, he was taken to court, where, as no tools had been found on him, that charge was changed to that of vagrancy, for which he was duly fined. All this enraged our hero so that he . . . well, can you guess what he did? He joined the Force and became a policeman. 'For great ideas let fools contest,' he said. 'If you can't love them, and want to do something about it, join them. All able-bodied, honest young dreamers should join the police, or become prison warders, or mental hospital nurses.'

Open the doors

I would have loved to be able to end this story by telling you that he has become a great reformer who has helped to open some hermetically closed doors. Alas, this is a true story, not a parable, and it ends with an anticlimax. He didn't last long in the police force. After a year or so, he resigned and is now a moderately successful businessman, buying and selling houses.

*

CODA

As you see, my Logic is not axiomatic. She doesn't march forward, goose-step by goose-step, from indubitable truths to indisputable consequences, from arbitrary principles to conclusions unchecked by results, deaf to the feedback of reality. It is empirical evidence rather than theoretical prejudice that shaped her body and guided her syllogisms.

Looking backwards over her shoulder, from the results towards the reasons, which were the results of previous reasons, she may never arrive at first principles, but, somewhere half-way along the chain of events, half-way between Man and the first nucleic acid molecules replicating themselves, she comes across a fact; not across a truth, but across a fact. A

Facts are beyond controversy, 'truths' are not

very simple fact. The fact that of all possible species of carnivora, those only survived whose everyhungry members did *not* devour their own children before the children grew up and produced the next and next and next carnivorous generation.

Ethics
is
physics

This illogical behaviour, which allowed the species to continue, you may call 'a biological fact', or you may call it 'altruism' or – why not? – 'love'. If you call it 'a biological fact', then it's physics. If you call it 'love', then it's ethics. And, in the cruel world, in which the beast had to attack to feed not only himself but also his litter, this biological fact, this logical absurdity, this unselfish quirk of DNA, this love, must have preceded aggression (which paradoxically, it caused) and thus decency must have preceded wickedness.

Progress

As time marches on, this logical absurdity of caring not only for himself makes the beast enlarge the field of decency from the litter to the pack, the tribe, race, class, nation, the whole species? Anyway, such a sequence of events is what I would like to call 'Progress'. And I would like to think that it is carried forward not by beliefs in fetishes, not by Great Illusions, not by aggression (WHICH, FROM BEING AGGRESSION FOR THE SAKE OF FOOD, DEGENERATED INTO AGGRESSION FOR THE SAKE OF IDEAS), but by its own evolutionary momentum. In spite of our cultural push-pulls, exercised by Grand Aims, noble or wicked.

*

When my Logic looks backwards over her shoulder, she sees that the absence of wicked means *is* more important than the presence of Grand Aims.

And when she turns around and glances forward into the future, what she sees is the urgent need for the food of common decencies, which will grow not from the aggressive nightmares of bygones, nor from the glorious blue-prints for the morrow, but from the common decencies of now.

***

EDITOR'S NOTES

1. Nick Wadley's introductory essay, 'Lines & Words & The Themersons,' first appeared in Ilona Haberstadt's elegant film appreciation review PIX1, London, Winter 1993/4, and was reprinted in *Critics and My Talking Dog,* Black River Falls, Wisconsin: Obscure Publications, 2001.

2. 'The Aim of Aims' (1978) is the first of two prose texts in this collection which also appeared in verse. As verse, 'The Aim of Aims' (and several other poems with a similar theme), was read by the author at literary events in London, Paris and Amsterdam, and is included in *Collected Poems,* Amsterdam: Gaberbocchus Press/De Harmonie, 1998. This prose version was previously published in *Six Short Texts,* Obscure Publications, 2004.

3. Written in the late 1940s or 1950s, 'Man's Superiority to the Beasts,' was published for the first time in OP's *Six Short Texts.* The corrected typescript of the text ends with a comma, but the manuscript suggests that this is the conclusion.

4. In May 1957, Stefan and Franciszka spent five days on holiday in Portbou and Cadaqués, Spain. Stefan bought a notebook and wrote 'Cadaqués' (1957), caricaturing a theological debate with a local priest. And Franciszka filled a sketchbook with 16 drawings, made with colored crayons, of that place and time. They left via

Figueras after visiting Salvador Dalí, as alluded to in the essay. The only previous publication of this text (together with Franciszka's Cadaqués drawings) was in *Cadaqués,* Obscure Publications, 2010.

5. 'Sketches from a Polite Hell' (1959) also was first published in OP's *Six Short Texts.* There is a similar play with language in Stefan's 'Meet another philosopher', which appeared as a prose poem in *Collected Poems,* with a slightly revised version serving as the coda to his story 'The Finishing School.' Stefan wrote the following introductory remarks for 'Sketches from a Polite Hell' in December 1959:

'Ladies and Gentlemen,

I have been asked to say anything that pleases me even if it does not please you. This is it.

There are some people in various countries who seem to be irritated by the difference which has developed between languages as they are spoken and the same languages as they are written.

The solution they usually choose is to change the way of writing so that what you see on paper would agree with the sound heard by your ear.

In England, for instance, George Bernard Shaw wanted to promote the invention of a systematic phonetic alphabet; in France, par example, Monsieur Raymond Queneau makes haphazard attempts to amuse readers by writing down some jokes the way they are spoken by some vulgar French people.

My idea is the opposite. I suggest that instead of making people write as they speak, we should try to make them pronounce as we spell, and this is an example of how this idea would sound in practice.'

6. Stefan dictated 'On fathers, wet-nurses and wars . . .' to Nick during July and August, 1988. Stefan also corrected the first three pieces, adding many question marks, translations, and asides. Nick added a note in the penultimate paragraph of the first piece. These four autobiographical fragments, together with an introductory essay and a Stefan Themerson bibliography by Nick, appeared in *Comparative Criticism,* volume 12, edited by E.S. Shaffer, Cambridge: Cambridge University Press, 1990.

7. It is not entirely certain when 'Critics and My Talking Dog' was written. Nick's bibliography, cited above, listed it as being written in 1958, but it could have been written somewhat earlier. The author provided most of the translations from the French but where they were lacking in the typescript, Barbara Wright graciously supplied them as indicated. The story was unpublished prior to its appearance in OP's *Critics and My Talking Dog.*

8. 'Castor and Pollux' (1954) is the other text in this collection which has appeared both in prose and verse. The verse version was included in *Collected Poems.* This prose version was first published as part of OP's *Six Short Texts.*

9. 'He was 47 or 48' was written in 1957 or 1958, and was unpublished prior to its inclusion in OP's *Six Short Texts.*

10. 'Chapter 18' was one of twenty chapters in the collaborative novel *London Consequences,* edited by Margaret Drabble and B.S.

Johnson, London: Greater London Arts Association, 1972. The editors wrote the first and last chapters, then provided an outline of the two main characters to the other authors, who wrote his or her chapter and passed the growing manuscript on to the next author. The book didn't identify which author wrote each particular chapter. Other authors in the group included Rayner Heppenstall, Paul Ableman, and Wilson Harris. OP reprinted the chapter by Stefan, with two talking dogs, in *The Finishing School and Chapter 18,* Obscure Publications, 2005.

11. 'The Finishing School, or Who from Whom?' was first published in the journal *Studio International,* volume 195, number 993/4, London, 1982. A slightly different version of the coda appeared as a prose poem in *Collected Poems.* OP included the story as part of its chapbook *The Finishing School and Chapter 18.*

12. Stefan wrote 'The Bone in the Throat', his only work in dramatic form, in 1959. A short excerpt was published that year in the initial issue of *New Departures,* an Oxford literary magazine, edited by Michael Horovitz. Among the other distinguished contributors to that issue were William Burroughs, Piero Heliczer, Stevie Smith, Kurt Schwitters, Patrick Bowles, and Samuel Beckett. Despite being called "a tremendously intelligent and clever and often very funny and original play" by London play agent Peggy Ramsay, the complete work remained unpublished until its appearance in *The Bone in the Throat,* Obscure Publications, 2007. The text of the OP edition was a 1964 revision marked "final."

13. On September 26, 1957, Stefan gave a talk, 'The Circle of Art and Science', as part of a regular Thursday evening program at the Gaberbocchus Common Room. The text was published in *ETC.: A*

Review of General Semantics, vol. XVI, no.3, San Francisco, Spring 1959. Operating in the basement beneath the Gaberbocchus Press office, the Common Room was intended to be a congenial place for artists and scientists to meet and exchange thoughts, play chess, look at journals and art works, hear talks or musical performances, watch scientific films, and enjoy spaghetti and wine. Franciszka's 1957 talk is reprinted as 'Bi-Abstract Pictures' in Nick Wadley's just released book, *Franciszka Themerson.* Subscribers (one guinea) could attend events on Thursdays, later on Tuesdays too. The Common Room was launched in August 1, 1957 and closed on July 9, 1959, after hosting 82 events.

14. In May 1963, Stefan delivered his lecture 'La Géometrie de la Satire', in French, at a conference on "Satira è Libertà Civili", in Conegliano (Veneto), Italy. The conference was organized by the literary review *Il Caffè* (Rome), which published nine texts by Stefan, including translated excerpts from *Bayamus, Professor Mmaa's Lecture,* 'The Bone in the Throat', and *St Francis and the Wolf of Gubbio* in the years between 1961 and 1970. Moderated by Roger Caillois, other conference participants included Raymond Queneau, Polish playwright Sławomir Mrożek, and Italian poets Giuseppe Ungaretti, Vittorio Sereni, and Carlo Betocchi. Barbara Wright translated the text of Stefan's talk for inclusion in *Geometry of Satire and Non Sequitur,* Obscure Publications, 2009.

15. 'The Chair of Decency' was the Huizinga-lecture given by Stefan in 1981 and published in a bi-lingual edition (with a Dutch translation and the original English text) in *Een Leerstoel in Fatsoen/ The Chair of Decency,* Amsterdam: Athenaeum-Polak & Van Gennep, 1982. OP reprinted Stefan's text in *The Chair of Decency,* Obscure Publications, 2007. For the OP edition, Jasia Reichardt generously

wrote the following introduction:

THE HUIZINGA LECTURE

At the end of February 1981, Stefan Themerson received a letter from A.S. Spoor, the editor-in-chief of *NRC Handelsblad* in Rotterdam, as follows:

"Dear Mr. Themerson,

Since 1972, when we celebrated the centenary of Johan Huizinga's, the famous Dutch historian, birthday in Leiden, the University of Leiden organises, together with the Nederlandse Maatschappij voor Letterkunde and the Dutch Daily NRC Handelsblad, annual lectures, called "Huizinga-lectures", in honour of Johan Huizinga. Alternately, the lectures are given by a Dutch and a foreign lecturer.

The first Huizinga-lecture took place on December 8, 1972. The Dutch author and essayist Rudy Kousbrock spoke about ethnology and cultural philosophy. In the years thereafter we had Mary McCarthy; the Dutch publicist Jan Pen; the French essayist and philosopher, Jean François Revel; the Dutch historian and biographer of Bakunin, Arthur Lehning; professor Noam Chomsky; the Dutch author Karel van het Reve; professor Golo Mann; and professor E.H. Kossman. We shall be proud to be able to add your name to this list as the lecturer for 1981."

Furthermore, Stefan learned that the lecture would be published in a brochure, and that after the lecture he would be invited to the customary "Huizinga-buffet-supper" at Spoor's house. Other invitees were to include the previous speakers, friends from universities, writers, members of NRC Handelsblad staff, and perhaps a few politicians.

The lectures were always on a Friday in December, and Stefan's talk was to be on December 11th.

Stefan accepted, and called his talk 'The Chair of Decency'. He sent the text of his talk on 28 October 1981 so that it could be published in advance. When a lady from Leiden telephoned him to find out what the lecture was about, and how to describe it on the invitation, Stefan wrote that he couldn't answer the question and could she ask Mr. Spoor to enlighten her.

The lecture took place in a church and Stefan recalled that at one point the bells rang, unannounced, to celebrate the occasion.

The lecture appeared in Dutch translation in *NRC Handelsblad* on 12 December 1981, and a small booklet published by Athenaeum-Polak & Van Gennep, Amsterdam in 1982. The Dutch translation was republished in an edition of the first fifteen Huizinga lectures, *Alle Cultuur is Streven,* Amsterdam, 1987.

Regrettably, A.S. Spoor's introduction to Stefan Themerson's lecture was mislaid in his office, Stefan never saw it, and has not been published.

The theme of *The Chair of Decency* – posing our innate biological goodness against the dangerous influence of culture and beliefs – is both a culmination and a précis of Themerson's thought and attitude. It runs through his lifetime of writing, in novels, essays and poems. Besides *The Chair of Decency,* the theme was crystallised in 'The Aim of Aims', sometimes presented as prose and sometimes as a poem.

Themerson concluded that Means are more important than Aims, that they should in fact BE the Aims. Aims are cultural, he said, but the proper Means are biological.

ABOUT THE AUTHOR

Stefan Themerson (born, 1910 – died, 1988), an avant-garde photographer, film-maker, philosopher, writer, and publisher, was born in Płock, Poland, then part of the Russian Empire. More interested in art and science than pursuing academic studies, he met and married Franciszka Weinles, a visual artist, in Warsaw, 1931. Together, they wrote and illustrated books for children and made five experimental films in Poland, before moving to Paris in the winter of 1937-38. With the start of World War II, Stefan joined the Polish Army in France, and Franciszka became a map-maker for the Polish Government-in-Exile and was evacuated to London. In 1942, he was reunited with her in London, after spending a couple of years in a refugee camp and a hostel in southern France. During this separation, he began his novel about termite civilization, *Professor Mmaa's Lecture*. Stefan became friends with Kurt Schwitters, and later, Bertrand Russell. In 1948, Stefan and Franciszka founded Gaberbocchus Press, which published many of Stefan's novels, including *Bayamus*, which introduced his Semantic Poetry, as well as the first English translations of Alfred Jarry and Raymond Queneau (translated by Barbara Wright). From 1957 to 1959, the Themersons operated the Gaberbocchus Common Room, in their Maida Vale flat, as a venue for readings, films, music recitals, and talks. They eventually transferred their press to a Dutch publisher in 1979. Stefan and Franciszka died, within a few months of each other, in 1988.

More Good Scat

For more information, visit **BlackScatBooks.com**